DRAWN *by* BEAUTY

"The Christian worldview makes clear that the good, the beautiful, and the true are absolutely indivisible. And yet, the modern age can be rightly understood as the effort to divide the transcendentals. It is the responsibility of the thinking Christian to seek faithfully to recover the unity of the good, the beautiful, and the true. We should welcome all serious works that help Christians in this effort. Matt Capps has offered a particularly thoughtful and helpful argument, and for that we should be thankful.

—**R. Albert Mohler Jr.**, president,
The Southern Baptist Theological Seminary

"This book is what we've needed for a long time: a gospel-focused look at beauty, wonder, and awe that actually models those things by the writer and evokes them for the reader. This book will help you in your discipleship and will prompt you to see the things around you in a different way."

—**Russell Moore**, editor in chief, *Christianity Today*

"For much of the modern age, art and aesthetics have been relegated to the church basement. It is encouraging to find in this book our old friend beauty being taken out of the storage box, dusted off, and set in a proper place: at the forefront of Christian thinking and spiritual formation. *Drawn by Beauty* is a study written for those who are longtime adorers of beauty and for those who love her only lately. This book, and the beauties it looks upon, will draw readers closer to the ultimate source of all beauty."

—**Karen Swallow Prior**, PhD, author and lecturer

"As Matt Capps rightly notes in this book, the concept of beauty can feel ethereal and abstract. We all recognize that there is beauty in the world, but is there a way to measure or define it? More important, is there any 'practical' benefit to pursuing it? Capps answers these questions (and many more) by distilling rich resources from the Christian theological and philosophical tradition into an accessible introduction for theologians, pastors, and laypeople alike."

—**Brandon D. Smith**, chair, Herschel H. Hobbs School of
Theology and Ministry, and associate professor of theology
and early Christianity, Oklahoma Baptist University;
and cofounder of the Center for Baptist Renewal

"Church buildings should be more than multifunctional—even more so the people who worship in them, who are to do, and be, 'beautiful things' (see Mark 14:6) that faintly mirror and faithfully attest the beauty of the triune God's self-giving love. Matt Capps helpfully reminds us that experiences of beauty draw us out of ourselves toward something greater, toward the God who is greater than can be perceived, yet who graciously reveals himself in the cross and in the face of Christ. I particularly appreciated the emphasis on attending to beauty as a means of spiritual formation, 'smelling salts' that open the eyes of the heart."

—**Kevin J. Vanhoozer**, research professor of systematic theology, Trinity Evangelical Divinity School

"Matt Capps provides a rich and substantive approach to beauty in our world as a signpost pointing to the triune God, whose beauty dazzles and transforms us. Drawing from the deep wells of Scripture and the Christian tradition, his work taps into our yearning to become one with the beauty we encounter. A chest of oft-unexplored treasures!"

—**Trevin Wax**, vice president for resources and marketing, North American Mission Board, and visiting professor, Cedarville University

"For believers living in an age drowning in entertainment but still diminished in wonder, Matt Capps's *Drawn by Beauty* is a course corrective with deep discernment and a keen understanding of Christianity's theological heritage of aesthetics. This book is as challenging as it is compelling, and it will draw readers into a more resonant faith, one that more gloriously adorns our glorious God."

—**Jared C. Wilson**, assistant professor of pastoral ministry and author in residence at Midwestern Seminary; pastor for preaching at Liberty Baptist Church, Liberty, Missouri

DRAWN *by* BEAUTY

Awe and Wonder in the Christian Life

MATTHEW Z. CAPPS

ACADEMIC®
BRENTWOOD, TENNESSEE

Drawn by Beauty: Awe and Wonder in the Christian Life

Published by B&H Academic®
Brentwood, Tennessee

ISBN: 978-1-0877-8710-7

Dewey Decimal Classification: 231.7
Subject Heading: AESTHETICS \ CREATION \ BIBLICAL COSMOLOGY

Cover design by Emily Keafer Lambright. Cover image by Jelena Markovic/ Stocksy.

Printed in the United States of America

30 29 28 27 26 25 VP 1 2 3 4 5 6 7 8 9 10

CONTENTS

PREFACE

> Beauty is the word that shall be our first. Beauty is the last thing which the thinking intellect dares to approach, since only it dances as an uncontained splendor around the double constellation of the true and good and their inseparable relation to one another.
>
> —*Hans Urs von Balthasar*, The Glory of the Lord: A Theological Aesthetics

This quote by the inimitable Hans Urs von Balthasar is daunting enough for me to ask myself, How dare I write a theological book on beauty, aesthetics, and spiritual formation? I certainly do not count myself in the same class as the brilliant minds who have produced complex but clarifying works in their years of reflection on these topics. In fact, there have been plenty of moments that I have wondered if my feeble attempt to approach these matters would be seen as sophomoric. I mean this with all sincerity. This is not some vain attempt to veil my pride in false humility. Topics like these are ethereal, often seemingly unapproachable. And writing this has been intimidating but also enlivening.

These topics have accompanied me in my own spiritual journey for over a decade. It all began when Professor John Hammett permitted me to go beyond the predetermined topics for a research paper and write on "a theology of beauty" in a master's level systematic theology course at Southeastern Baptist Theological Seminary. His constructive criticism reminded me that I had only begun my journey. Later in the doctoral program at Gordon-Conwell Theological Seminary, these subjects became the focus of my thesis project under Steve Klipowicz and David Currie. Much of that research became the foundation of the book you hold in your hands. Beyond these seasons of formal research, theological reflections on beauty and aesthetics have functioned in my mind like the unseen programs running in the background of a computer. Always there, if not always at the forefront. Such is the nature of a curious mind.

This curiosity has regularly led me to sit at the feet of theological giants like Augustine, Thomas Aquinas, Jonathan Edwards, and Hans Urs von Balthasar—among others. Indeed, the early church father and philosopher Augustine was among the vanguard in approaching the field of aesthetics from a distinctly Christian perspective. While one of Augustine's earliest treatises on beauty has been lost, titled *On the Beautiful and Fitting,* his major contributions in the field of aesthetics can be found throughout his other writings as his existential journey of faith was indispensable to developing his ideas on these subjects.[1]

Like Augustine before him, medieval Italian philosopher and theologian Thomas Aquinas is also a prominent figure in

---

[1] See John Navone, *Toward a Theology of Beauty* (Collegeville, MN: Liturgical, 1996), 54.

discussions of beauty and aesthetics. While Aquinas never neatly organized a discourse on beauty or aesthetics, he did present these topics as a self-contained and coherent component within his larger philosophical system in relation to the triune God.[2]

Jonathan Edwards, who is also arguably one of the most highly regarded protestant theologians, also contributed to the field of theological aesthetics. Beauty is a fundamental theme in Edwards's understanding of being and genuine religious experience.[3] Indeed, Edwardsian scholarship has noted that he "regarded beauty as fundamental to his understanding of God."[4]

Finally, Swiss theologian Hans Urs von Balthasar, widely recognized as one of the greatest Roman Catholic theologians of the twentieth century, wrote extensively in the field of theological aesthetics. The centerpiece of Balthasar's theology is his theological trilogy: *The Glory of the Lord*, *Theo-Drama*, and *Theo-Logic*. Some have called *The Glory of the Lord* his "theo-aesthetics." While that is not the title Balthasar chose, it does capture the essence of his work in this field.

There are vast riches to be mined in the Christian tradition regarding beauty and aesthetics. Throughout church history, discussions on aesthetics and beauty have varied "from murmur

---

[2] Andreas Speer, "Thomas Aquinas," in *Encyclopedia of Aesthetics*, vol. 1, ed. Michael Kelly (New York: Oxford University Press, 1998), 77.

[3] See Roland Delattre, *Beauty and Sensibility in the Thought of Jonathan Edwards: An Essay in Aesthetics and Theological Ethics* (Eugene, OR: Wipf and Stock, 2006), 1.

[4] Michael J. McClymond and Gerald R. McDermott, *The Theology of Jonathan Edwards* (New York: Oxford University Press, 2012), 93.

to roar."[5] This variation is unfortunate because every Christian would benefit from the practice of "theological retrieval," to guard against the self-imposed amnesia that epitomizes many popular thinkers and cultural tastemakers today, even in Christianity.[6] In this work, what I present is both a survey and a summary. Because I stand on the shoulders of theological giants, you will certainly hear substantial echoes of others, both conscious and subconscious.

While writing this, I was often reminded of Eccl 1:9 because the discussion of beauty and aesthetics has spanned time and continents. Nevertheless, I present this work as my own contribution, with my own distinct composition and reflection, but I have not covered everything. After all, this is meant to be an introductory albeit reflective book. Moreover, I have followed the advice of C. S. Lewis, who advised a young writer to "take great pains to be clear."[7] My aim was to write in a way that is conversant with the academy but is also useful for pastors, leaders, and thoughtful laity of the church—especially Christian artisans. The first two chapters introduce what we are talking about and why we are talking about it. The next six chapters broadly follow the categories of systematic theology—the

---

[5] Stephen Garrett, *Beauty and the Baptists*, 2 (paper presented at the Young Scholars in the Baptist Academy Seminar, 2006), https://www.academia.edu/2073444/Beauty_and_the_Baptists.

[6] See Gavin Ortlund's *Theological Retrieval for Evangelicals: Why We Need Our Past to Have a Future* (Wheaton, IL: Crossway, 2019). See C. S. Lewis, *Surprised by Joy* (London: Geoffrey Bles, 1955).

[7] See C. S. Lewis's letter to a girl named Thomasine (December 14, 1959), who once inquired of Lewis for writing advice in his *Words to Live By: A Guide for the Merely Christian* (New York: HarperCollins, 2007), 310.

doctrines of revelation, God, Christ, man, and last things in relation to beauty. The last two chapters offer reflections on spiritual formation and art.

Soli Deo Gloria
Matthew Z. Capps

ACKNOWLEDGMENTS

I am thankful for my beloved wife, Laura, who didn't bemoan my late nights at my garage desk working on this project. She has been a constant source of encouragement and, when needed, the voice of motivation. My children, Solomon, Ruby, and Abby, have always motivated me to pursue excellence in all things. My parents introduced me to the arts and paved the way for my enjoyment of them. The members of Fairview Baptist Church, where I pastor, have also demonstrated generosity and support as I have devoted energy to this book. I owe a debt of gratitude to Benjamin Quinn, who extended the invitation to publish this book after conversations at a Templeton Foundation-funded cohort with the Center for Faith and Culture at Southeastern Baptist Theological Seminary. To the team at B&H Academic, Logan Pyron and Michael McEwen, who served as the sub/content editors of this book; Jessi Wallace as the managing editor; and Madison Trammel as the publisher. These brothers and sisters refined this work so that it could be presented to you in its final form. Finally, I offer this work in worshipful response to my God, who is the source and substance of all true beauty. To Jesus Christ, in whom I will eventually behold divine beauty "face to face." And to the Holy Spirit, who has opened my eyes to be enraptured by the beauty of trinitarian delight.

1

A Meditation on a Seashore

Waking Up to the Beauty around Us

Great are you, O Lord, and exceedingly worthy of praise; your power is immense, and your wisdom beyond reckoning. And so we men, who are a due part of your creation, long to praise you—we also carry our mortality about with us, carry the evidence of our sin and with it the proof that you thwart the proud. You arouse us so that praising you may bring us joy, because you have made us and drawn us to yourself, and our heart is restless until it rests in you.

—*Augustine*, Confessions

Beauty and Aesthetics

Finally Seeing at the Sea

Though it was over a decade ago, it was as if it had happened yesterday. I didn't want that experience to end. And in some ways, it never did.

It was an invigorating early fall morning on the North Carolina coast. I, along with two friends, had rented a beachfront house to celebrate the final semester of our master's level seminary studies. The weather that morning hovered in the high sixties and highlighted the fragrant black coffee on my leisurely stroll down the vacant beach at sunrise. The soothing roar of the vast ocean was a reminder of its constant, surging strength. Its sparkling swells crashed into the shore and cooled the sand on my bare feet. The vibrant colors of the sky provided a breathtaking background for the innumerable cumulus clouds that slowly hovered across the eastern shoreline. I was exhilarated by the warmth of the sun's rays merging with the crisp, salty air. Unbeknownst to me, that morning walk would be the beginning of an unexpected and profound spiritual and intellectual journey. It was as if my soul had finally and fully opened to the enrapturing power of beauty.

In many ways this moment was ironic. As a child, I enjoyed private lessons in the classical arts and excelled in the arts throughout grade school. Not only is my father an artist, but I also earned an undergraduate degree in the arts. My aesthetic sensibilities were cultivated toward maturity from a very early age. Nevertheless, on that day at the beach, as one who had almost "mastered" divinity, I found myself struggling for a theological framework to process this ethereal seashore experience of the breathtaking work of God's hands. In seminary I was trained to defend Christian truth and advocate for the good of Christian ethics, but I was unsure of what to do with the experience of beauty.

As I absorbed all that was around me on the beach at daybreak—the sights, the sounds, the touches—it stirred a yearning within me that I could hardly put into words. It is a sensation that I imagine you have felt as well. Perhaps you have experienced it when stilled on the precipice of the Grand Canyon, where everything is dwarfed and all sounds are swallowed.[1] Maybe you have perceived it when overwhelmed by awe standing before a Renaissance master's magnum opus. It is in the peaceful tranquility of witnessing beams of light cut through the dense canopy of forest treetops. It can be found in the melodic moments of an intimate and introspective song that whisks you away in hopeful yearning or pulls you into a poignant moment from the past. This is the power of beauty. A power that is universal and so recognizable that even one of the most strident atheists has argued, "When you consider the beauty of the world . . . you are naturally overwhelmed with a feeling of awe, a feeling of admiration, and you almost feel a desire to worship something."[2]

The Undeniable Aesthetic Allure

Beauty demands to be noticed. After all, can any person truly deny the reality of beauty in the created world? Can anyone refute the perception of aesthetic delight in human experience? As English philosopher Roger Scruton once observed, "[Beauty] is never viewed with indifference. . . . It speaks to us directly

---

[1] This wording is adapted from author Bill Bryson's description in *The Lost Continent: Travels in Small Town America* (New York: Harper and Row, 1989), 237.

[2] Pangambam S, "FULL TRANSCRIPT: The God Delusion Debate—Richard Dawkins vs John Lennox," *Singju Post*, July 6, 2023, https://singjupost.com/full-transcript-the-god-delusion-debate-richard-dawkins-vs-john-lennox/.

like the voice of an intimate friend."[3] The voice of beauty elicits a sense of longing, "the kind of pleasure which is exquisite and yet leaves us unsatisfied."[4] These glorious but fleeting moments of aesthetic delight tend to slip through our fingers. We ache for more. There is an aesthetic desire in all of us, an appetite that cannot be sated, at least not fully, in the present age. C. S. Lewis portrays this hunger produced by our aesthetic appetite quite poignantly: "We do not want merely to see beauty, though, God knows, even that is bounty enough. We want something else which can hardly be put into words—to be united with the beauty we see, to pass into it, to receive it into ourselves, to bathe in it, to become part of it."[5]

What are we to do when beauty excites a sensation that deepens our curiosity?[6] Once we have bathed in beauty and have been awakened by its enchantment, what then? If "beauty is both something that calls us out of ourselves and something which appeals to feelings deep within us," where do we turn from there?[7] These questions haunted me after that coastal autumn morning. On the one hand, I had discovered

---

[3] Roger Scruton, *Beauty: A Very Short Introduction* (New York: Oxford University Press, 2009), ix.

[4] N. T. Wright, *Simply Christian: Why Christianity Makes Sense* (New York: Harper One, 2006), 41.

[5] Preached originally as a sermon in the Church of St. Mary the Virgin, Oxford, on June 8, 1942, and published later in *The Weight of Glory* (San Francisco: Harper, 2001), 16–17.

[6] C. S. Lewis often described the experience of beauty with the German word *Sehnsucht*, a noun meaning "longing," "craving," or "yearning." See, for example, Lewis, *Surprised by Joy: The Shape of My Early Life* (New York: Harcourt, Brace, 1955), 5; and *The Pilgrim's Regress* (Grand Rapids: Eerdmans, 2014), 106.

[7] Wright, *Simply Christian*, 44.

that a greater appreciation of beauty and aesthetic experience is something worthy of deep contemplation, an affection to be cultivated. On the other hand, I began to ponder the ways beauty and aesthetics could serve as a signpost pointing beyond the experience itself. Perhaps to something, even Someone else? As with any aesthetic delight that temporarily nourishes the soul, beauty itself will not benefit us in the long run if it does not get us to its final end.[8] So I needed to chart a path for this journey.

Perhaps you have never slowed down long enough to truly reflect on the properties of beauty. Maybe you have never pondered the deep and moving power of aesthetic experiences. This is the reason I wrote this book. Disciplined study will often unearth appropriate words and concepts to help us understand such exalted aesthetic experiences. As Jeremy Begbie writes, "When we learn another language for the first time, we discover more about the world. . . . When an Eskimo gives me a huge range of words for 'snow,' each referring to a different type, my perception of snow is enriched—I see more than I saw before."[9] To begin, while we will go further up and deeper in throughout this work, allow me to initially, and succinctly, define three concepts that are central to our inquiry: beauty, aesthetics, and spiritual formation. In doing this, I will also welcome you into the conversations related to our subjects and introduce you to the Christian thinkers who have led these discussions in the past.

---

[8] See John-Mark L. Miravalle, *Beauty: What It Is and Why It Matters* (Manchester, NH: Sophia Institute, 2019), 111.

[9] Jeremy Begbie, *Beholding the Glory* (Grand Rapids: Baker, 2001), xi.

The Vocabulary of Beauty and Aesthetics

What is beauty? This is a question that stretches back centuries. A powerful unanimity prevailed concerning the general characteristics of beauty from the early Hellenists to the eighteenth century. Essentially, there were four categories in which beauty had been described or explained.[10] First, the classical description called "the Great Theory of Beauty" understands beauty as consisting in a harmony of parts to a whole—harmony, proportion, and unity—what could also be called fittingness.[11] A second category follows Plato in describing beauty as one of the "transcendentals," among truth and goodness. For Platonic thinkers, beauty is understood as the radiance of truth and goodness.[12] As we will see, the great Platonic theory of beauty was given a Christian reformulation in Augustine and Aquinas, among others. A third description of beauty, which is most attentive to subjectivity, affirms that "whatever beauty itself is, to experience it is pleasurable."[13] To put it plainly, beauty could be described as that which is pleasing at the very apprehension of it, to paraphrase Thomas Aquinas.[14] Fourth, some Christian theologians take God as the source and substance of true beauty. In other words, this

---

[10] See David Bentley Hart, *The Beauty of the Infinite: The Aesthetics of Christian Truth* (Grand Rapids: Eerdmans, 2004), 17. See also Edward Craig, *Routledge Encyclopedia of Philosophy*, vol. 1 (New York: Routledge, 1998), 680.

[11] See Edward Farley, *Faith and Beauty: A Theological Aesthetic* (Aldershot, UK: Ashgate, 2001), 17.

[12] See Stratford Caldecott, *Beauty for Truth's Sake: On the Re-Enchantment of Education* (Grand Rapids: Brazos, 2009), 31.

[13] Jeremy Begbie, *Beholding the Glory*, 17.

[14] See Thomas Aquinas, *Summa Theologica*, I, q. 5, art. 4, ad. 1.

fourth approach to beauty holds that beauty is the sum of God's attributes—the radiance of his very being. Thus, beauty is seen as the outward expression of God's very self. In the words of James S. Spiegel, "All that is beautiful either *is* him or comes *from* him."[15]

Descriptions abound, but beauty remains something of an enigma. While various thinkers have offered descriptive observations regarding beauty, David Bentley Hart has argued that it is impossible for anyone to offer a conclusive definition of beauty.[16] In the words of Dostoevsky, "Beauty is a fearful and terrible thing! Fearful because it's undefinable, and it cannot be defined, because here God gave us only riddles."[17] In some cases, the general concepts of beauty do not always hold when considering all the delightful experiences or works of art. However, within the Christian tradition it is agreed upon that beauty is both objectively real and subjectively experienced.[18] It can also be argued that the subjective experience granted in beauty is universal.

This universal experience encountered in beauty is explored in what would be called the field of aesthetics. Concerning aesthetics, an enlightenment philosopher in the eighteenth century by the name of Alexander Gottlieb Baumgarten coined the term for modern thinkers in his 1750 tract *Aesthetica*.

---

[15] James S. Spiegel, "Aesthetics and Worship," *Southern Baptist Journal of Theology* 2, no. 4 (1998): 42.

[16] Hart, *The Beauty of the Infinite*, 15.

[17] Fyodor Dostoevsky, *The Brothers Karamazov*, trans. Richard Pevear and Larissa Volokhonsky (New York: Farrar, Straus and Giroux, 2002), pt. 1, bk. 3, 108.

[18] Jonathan King, *The Beauty of the Lord: Theology as Aesthetics* (Bellingham, WA: Lexham, 2018), 50.

Baumgarten "sought to understand how the human encounter with beauty might be rendered into something like a science unique in its own right and separate from other disciplines."[19] The word *aesthetics* is derived from the Greek root meaning "perception by the senses" or, more precisely, the general study of sensation or feeling.[20] Aesthetics is the science of sensuous knowledge, or our "sense appetites."[21] Anyone who has been given an anesthetic at the dentist can grasp the existential meaning of the term.

Whether we are conscious of it or not, we are constantly affected by the aesthetics of our surroundings in what we see, hear, and smell, and in the temperature and texture of the things we touch. Whether or not we find such experiences beautiful is often measured by our awe or delight. As Nicholas Wolterstorff notes, "In general it can be said that if in contemplating something for its own sake we get enjoyment out of how it looks or sounds, then we have aesthetic satisfaction."[22] Some who specialize in this field of study might make a distinction between the sensory experience of beauty itself and philosophical reflection and judgment rendered at the experience of beauty, but we will use the category

[19] Brendan Thomas Sammon, *Called to Attraction: An Introduction to the Theology of Beauty* (Eugene, OR: Wipf and Stock, 2017), 111.

[20] See Richard Viladesau, *Theological Aesthetics: God in Imagination, Beauty, and Art* (New York: Oxford University Press), 6–7.

[21] E. F. Carritt, ed. *Philosophies of Beauty: From Socrates to Robert Bridges* (Oxford: Clarendon, 1931), 84.

[22] Nicholas Wolterstorff, *Art in Action* (Grand Rapids: Eerdmans, 1996), 40.

of aesthetics broadly to examine the role of beauty in the life of faith.[23] In this sense, aesthetics is about forming a criticism of taste, a category of thought primarily occupied with the study of empirical sensation and reflection on beauty.[24] Thus, in some way, all inquiries into aesthetics involve the phenomenon of beauty.

In some cases, these two fields of aesthetics and beauty have been examined independently of one another. In other words, beauty has been thought of as "out there," a phenomenon independent of human cognition, while aesthetics has been thought of as perception "in here," within the experience of human consciousness.[25] However, within the Christian tradition, the two have generally been held together as interpenetrating one another. In the academy there are distinct branches of theological scholarship related to beauty and aesthetics.

---

[23] Note that when it comes to art, one of the defining aspects of the aesthetic experience in the modern world is the idea of "liking without wanting." German philosopher Immanuel Kant, in his *Critique of Judgement*, published in 1790, argued that the aesthetic experience is one of disinterested interest. In other words, we are interested because we enjoy art, but we are disinterested in that we do not want anything from it other than satisfaction. See Immanuel Kant, *Critique of the Power of Judgment*, trans. Paul Guyer and Eric Mathews, ed. Paul Guyer (Cambridge: Cambridge University Press, 2000), 96.

[24] James McCullough distinguishes between aesthesis (sensory reception that develops the imagination) and ascesis (athletic term adopted for disciplines associated with growth). See McCullough, *Sense and Spirituality: The Arts and Spiritual Formation* (Eugene, OR: Wipf and Stock, 2015).

[25] See Sammon, *Called to Attraction*, 4.

Protestant theologian Jonathan King outlines four distinct theological approaches in this field of study.[26] First, a *natural theology of aesthetics* seeks to give an account from the perceivable beauty of the natural world in light of the Christian God. Second, *a theology of the arts* aims to understand the place of the arts in the formation of Christians. Third, *religious aesthetics* attempts to understand the aesthetic phenomena in art and the natural world in relation to Christian practices. Finally, *theological aesthetics* relates beauty to the attributes of God revealed through both general and special revelation. While these are complex and diverse fields of doctrinal discourse, we will utilize the insights of each broadly in this introductory reflection on these topics.

What of Beauty, Aesthetics, and Spiritual Formation?

The goal of this book is to connect the topics of beauty and aesthetics to spiritual formation. My aim is to help you move beyond sensory experience and philosophical speculation to develop a more distinctly Christian understanding of beauty and aesthetics from a theological perspective for our spiritual formation. Understanding aesthetics is not so much a "theological option as a theological necessity" for all Christians.[27] You might be thinking, *I am no theologian*. I can understand that sentiment if you have never received formal theological training;

---

[26] See King, *The Beauty of the Lord*, 2–7.

[27] Frank Burch Brown, *Religious Aesthetics: A Theological Study of Making and Meaning* (Princeton, NJ: Princeton University Press, 1990), 37.

however, it is widely held that all Christians are theologians in some sense. The difference between a lay theologian and a professional theologian is one of degree, not kind.[28] As Graeme Goldsworthy explains, "Every Christian by definition knows God, thinks about God and makes statements about God. . . . Part of being a Christian is that we do theology."[29] We cannot get away from the task of theology because we cannot get away from God. Theology is inescapable because God is inevitable. The question we should ask ourselves is, Do we ponder carefully how all things relate to the triune God?

The same could be asked of beauty and aesthetics. As humans, we cannot escape the aesthetic task because the perception of beauty is universal to humankind and because aesthetic experiences form individuals, no matter their worldview. If the practice of aesthetics is the responsibility of every person, this is especially true for Christians. American Eastern Orthodox philosopher David Bentley Hart champions this notion vigorously: "Beauty is a category indispensable to Christian thought."[30] It's exactly on this point that one may defend the notion that Christian thinkers should be the true aesthetes.

Because my goal is to relate the topics of beauty and aesthetics to spiritual formation, much of our reflection will be tethered to Scripture and related to how we contribute to and experience the world around us, from meadows to museums.

---

[28] See Stanley Grenz and Roger Olson, *Who Needs Theology? An Invitation to the Study of God* (Wheaton, IL: InterVarsity, 1996).

[29] Graeme Goldsworthy, *According to Plan* (Downers Grove, IL: InterVarsity, 1991), 29.

[30] Hart, *The Beauty of the Infinite*, 16.

As with any subject of theological examination, Scripture holds forth propositions to contemplate. But those propositions also shape our practices and invite us to participate in God and his world. Thus, as we reflect on beauty and aesthetics in relation to spiritual formation, we are drawn into what Kevin J. Vanhoozer calls "theodramatic action" that elicits a response.[31] This idea of participating in the "theodrama" attempts to avoid the extremes of the traditional-cognitive and the experiential-expressive ways of developing our theology. To adapt the words of John Calvin, "the whole world is a theatre" for the display of God's beauty, and the church is called to play the part of the orchestra or the audience at different times and in different ways.[32] Therefore, we must learn to respond as biblical doctrine directs us, and our response—or theological enactment—is intimately connected to our beautification and our sanctification.

One of the reasons I have written this book is to help you "come to your senses." We all need to become aware of the beauty around us because the beauty around us also shapes us. The Protestant evangelical tradition has, until recently, largely neglected inquiry into beauty or aesthetics as they relate to spiritual formation. Peter Adam has contended that "many evangelical Christians are weary of the word 'spirituality' itself, fearing

---

[31] Kevin J. Vanhoozer, *The Drama of Doctrine: A Canonical Linguistic Approach to Christian Theology* (Louisville: WJK, 2005), 67. Vanhoozer's approach to theology attempts to navigate the nuances and complexities of the interdependent relationships among exegesis, doctrine, and practice.

[32] See John Calvin, *Commentary on the Book of Psalms. By John Calvin. Translated from the Original Latin, and Collated with the Author's French Version, by the Rev. James Anderson*, vol. 5. (Edinburgh: printed for the Calvin Translation Society, 1849), 178.

that is far removed from authentic faith and experience."[33] Alister E. McGrath rightly counters that "Christian spirituality concerns the quest for fulfilled and authentic Christian existence, involving the bringing together of the fundamental ideas of Christianity and the whole experience of living on the basis of and within the scope of the Christian faith."[34] After all, human beings are embodied creatures who are formed by not only their spiritual practices but also their affective experiences. In this sense, spiritual formation is a conversation between God's revelation and our reception, which includes our experiences, desires, and imaginations—all being shaped by the Spirit and the Christian tradition we find ourselves in.[35] Reflecting on the relationships among spiritual formation, beauty, and aesthetics actually shapes us *in* our spiritual formation.

Conclusion

As I learned on the North Carolina coast, experiencing beauty draws us beyond ourselves into an experience of something greater than ourselves. Beauty stirs us with longing, makes reality come into focus, and pierces us with a sense that things in

---

[33] See Peter Adam, *Hearing God's Words: Exploring Biblical Spirituality* (Downers Grove, IL: InterVarsity, 2004), 21.

[34] Alister E. McGrath, *Christian Spirituality: An Introduction* (Hoboken, NJ: Wiley-Blackwell, 1999), 2.

[35] James K. A. Smith, *Imagining The Kingdom: How Worship Works* (Grand Rapids: Baker, 2013), 15. It is important to note what is meant by imagination here; it does not mean fantasy but refers to a particular way of making sense of the world. See David I. Smith in *Teaching and Christian Practices: Reshaping Faith and Learning*, ed. James K. A. Smith and David I. Smith (Grand Rapids: Eerdmans, 2011), 211–23.

life actually matter. Aesthetic experiences have meaning and are to be treasured and explored. They serve as a sign, and they orient us in the quest for the real, for the world as it actually is, and for the hope of the world to come. After all, in a world without beauty, Balthasar declares, "What remains is then a mere lump of existence."[36] I believe Christians need to pursue the marvelous and to lean into the pursuit of beauty for the sake of their souls. It's lamentable, as Balthasar says, that "the idea of beauty" has "been reduced to that of a merely this-worldly aesthetics."[37]

My prayer is that, as you read, you will come to understand that the revelation of beauty is an act of God's self-revealing love.[38] The foundational theological assertion concerning beauty and aesthetics is that God alone is the infinite source and substance of true beauty. Not only were we crafted in his image as aesthetic creatures, but we are also endowed with the capacity to enjoy and cultivate beautiful things. Beauty forms us, and to neglect the beautiful in the Christian life is to fail to become the type of people fully alive to God and his purposes for the world. It is the highest spiritual calling in our journey of faith not only to grow in sound knowledge of truth, to faithfully reflect God's good character, but also to delight in his beauty. As Augustine

---

[36] Hans Urs von Balthasar, *The Glory of the Lord: A Theological Aesthetics*, vol. 1 (London: T&T Clark, 1982), 19.

[37] Aidan Nichols, *A Key to Balthasar: Hans Urs von Balthasar on Beauty, Goodness, and Truth* (Grand Rapids: Baker Academic, 2011), 12.

[38] In turn, drawing on Augustine, philosopher James K. A. Smith has often argued that we are shaped by the things toward which we orient our desires. We are what we love because we become what we behold. See James K. A. Smith's *You Are What You Love: The Spiritual Power of Habit* (Grand Rapids: Brazos, 2016) and *Desiring the Kingdom: Worship, Worldview, and Cultural Formation* (Grand Rapids: Baker Academic, 2009).

said, our hearts will be restless until they rest in him. While Christian theology can never fully capture the beauty of God, it can challenge us to think deeply and long more hopefully for God. Indeed, according to Steven J. Duby, "to undertake the Christian practice of pondering and speaking about God in himself is to have a foretaste of the eschatological joy into which Christ invites his people."[39] As Jonathan Edwards has taught us, "God is glorified not only by His glory's being seen, but by its being rejoiced in. When those that see it delight in it, God is more glorified than if they only see it. His glory is then received with the whole soul, both by the understanding and by the heart. God made the world that He might communicate, and the creature receive, His glory."[40]

---

[39] Steven J. Duby, *God in Himself: Scripture, Metaphysics, and the Task of Christian Theology* (Downers Grove, IL: InterVarsity, 2019), 10.

[40] Jonathan Edwards, "Miscellany #448," *The "Miscellanies," The Works of Jonathan Edwards*, ed. Thomas A. Schafer, vol. 13 (New Haven, CT: Yale University Press, 1994), 495.

2

The Echoes of Footsteps in Empty Rooms

Why Has Beauty Become a Theological Beast?

If the joys of heaven are for most of us in our
present condition an acquired taste, then
there are certain ways of life that may render
the taste impossible of acquisition.

Heaven offers nothing that the mercenary soul can
desire. It is safe to tell the pure of heart that they
will see God, for only the pure of heart want to. If
we find in ourselves a desire which no experience in
this world can satisfy, the most probable explanation
is that we were made for another world.

—*John Navone*, Enjoying God's Beauty

What Happened to Aesthetics in the Church?

As our mission team circled the last hill in our springtime drive through the countryside of Hungary, the magnificent Károlyi Palace began to peek over the horizon. Our guides, Alicia and László, had scheduled a late afternoon tour of this late Renaissance-style palace for our team as the conclusion to our week of mission work in the nearby villages. As we walked through the manicured garden path toward the stairway to the arched entry doors, I reflected on the architectural contrast of this historical landmark against the day-to-day living quarters of those we had ministered to the days before. Inside, the charming décor and exquisitely crafted furniture in each room were a vestige of the past, the left-behind remnants of the affluent family that resided in a vastly different world than those who lived and worked in the valley below them. It was not difficult to imagine the luxurious lifestyle the wealthy owners once enjoyed, not unlike the animated princess movies that my young daughters regularly enjoy. However, the classical portraits that adorned the towering walls were all that remained of the individuals who, at some point, had inhabited each room. Our tour ended as the sun began to set, and the mansion prepared to close for the evening.

As we headed down toward the valley, I reflected on our experience and how it mirrored the modern church's relationship with beauty and aesthetics. In many ways, beauty and aesthetics are topics that are briefly and only occasionally visited, and they are beyond the normal spiritual vocabulary of most Christians. These two topics have become nothing more than the echoes of footsteps in empty rooms. The result is that far too many Christians are aesthetically impoverished and weary of beauty, fearing that these subjects are far removed from authentic faith and day-to-day practice.[1] The question is, Why has beauty become the theological beast? Why has it become Cinderella's stepsister to truth and goodness in the Christian life?[2]

In recent times, most of the contributions on beauty have come from trained specialists in the field of philosophy, namely those who concentrate primarily on aesthetics.[3] Even among those philosophers, beauty appears to be a shopworn subject, as many of them suggest that it "is a category we ought to discard altogether."[4] Religion and philosophy have often been called ancient siblings, and like siblings they've mimicked each other in how they treat the areas of beauty and aesthetics. It seems that many modern Christian thinkers have neglected the subjects of beauty and aesthetics just as much as their modern philosophical counterparts.[5] For the most part, Protestant

---

[1] See Hans Urs von Balthasar, *Word and Revelation* (New York: Herder and Herder, 1964), 162.

[2] See Patrick Sherry, *Spirit and Beauty: An Introduction to Theological Aesthetics* (London: SCM, 2002), 18.

[3] See David Bentley Hart, *The Beauty of the Infinite: The Aesthetics of Christian Truth* (Grand Rapids: Eerdmans, 2003), 15.

[4] R. Albert Mohler, *The Disappearance of God: Dangerous Beliefs in the New Spiritual Openness* (Colorado Springs: Multnomah, 2009), 49.

[5] A few exceptions would be Reformed theologian Herman Bavinck, who explores beauty and aesthetics in his work *Reformed Dogmatics*, vol. 2, *God and Creation* (Grand Rapids: Baker Academic, 2004), 254, 316; John Frame, who briefly discusses the beauty of God under the category of God's goodness in *Systematic Theology* (Phillipsburg, NJ: P&R, 2013), 253; and Wayne Grudem, who includes beauty as one of the communicable attributes of God in *Systematic Theology* (Grand Rapids: Zondervan, 1994), 219–20.

Christian tradition has been largely "silent, cryptic, or . . . inconclusive" on these matters.[6] Dorothy Sayers goes so far as to argue that "we have no Christian [a]esthetic . . . there have . . . been plenty of writers on [a]esthetics who happened to be Christians, but they seldom made any consistent attempt to relate their [a]esthetic to the central Christian dogmas."[7] Even if Sayers overstates her case, the concern is monumental enough to give us pause.[8]

It is no stretch to argue that the evangelical church has largely neglected theological inquiry into the nature of beauty and aesthetics, especially in their relation to spiritual formation. Yet for much of Christian history, such neglect has not always been the case. To understand where we stand today, it's important for us to look back to see why modern Protestant Christians have an underdeveloped appreciation or, perhaps, a dogged aversion to these wondrous and richly rewarding realities. In doing this, I would like to offer a few observations on our aesthetic malnutrition to frame our neglect of beauty and aesthetics in Christian spiritual formation. After all, ideas have consequences. And these consequences still haunt us today; we are still swimming and struggling against these undercurrents of thought.

---

[6] Frank Burch Brown, *Religious Aesthetics: A Theological Study of Making and Meaning* (Princeton, NJ: Princeton University Press, 1989), 17.

[7] Dorothy Sayers, *The Whimsical Christian: 18 Essays* (New York: Macmillan, 1978), 74.

[8] See Jeremy Begbie, *Voicing Creation's Praise: Toward a Theology of the Arts* (New York: T&T Clark, 1991), xv.

Six Undercurrents

The Untethered Fear of Idolatry

First, there is the religious tendency to overextend our healthy concern for idolatry and, in turn, legalistically attempt to avoid the alluring power of beauty altogether.[9] For this reason, there is a profound history of trepidation within the Judeo-Christian tradition regarding the danger of aesthetic experiences. The ancient Hebrews "developed a deep aversion to physical representations which *could* be interpreted as objects of worship."[10] After all, while the first commandment is against worshipping the wrong god, the second commandment is against worshipping the right God in the wrong way. Nevertheless, the prohibition against idolatry is not a condemnation of aesthetic admiration or the making of beautiful things but instead is a condemnation of worshipping anyone or anything other than the one true God. Consider the Israelites who fashioned a golden calf to worship (Exod 20:4–6; 32), or Paul's warning to the fools in Rome who exchanged the glory of the immortal God for images resembling mortal man: birds, four-footed animals, and reptiles (Rom 1:22–23). However, "the prohibition against graven images" was so deeply implanted in the people's consciousness that the

---

[9] For a helpful book-length treatment on the concept of idolatry in Scripture, see Gregory Beale, *We Become What We Worship: A Biblical Theology of Idolatry* (Eugene, OR: Wipf and Stock, 2020).

[10] Francis M. DuBose, *God Who Sends: A Fresh Quest for Biblical Mission* (Nashville: Broadman, 1983), 88. One could argue that aesthetics did play a significant role in the lives of ancient Israelites primarily in the composition of the Scriptures, whereby God's revelation and action are contemplated. See Gerhard Von Rad, *Old Testament Theology*, vol. 1 (Louisville: WJK, 2001), 65.

Israelites did not leave a legacy of beautiful artifacts comparable to their ancient contemporaries.[11] In the ancient Near East, much like today, the artistic embellishments representing many of the pagan religions remind us that they divinized everything from the sun to the stars to statues.

As for the Christian tradition, much could be said here, but it should suffice to say that the second commandment does not condemn the use of beautiful or aesthetically pleasing elements and embellishments in religious spaces, but it does prohibit infusing these elements with spiritual power, as to represent the immanence of God or bring us into a more intimate communion with him. The broader concept of idolatry is more complex than simply imaging or envisioning God apart from how he has revealed himself.[12] At a much deeper level, idola-

---

[11] See DuBose, *God Who Sends*, 88. Wilken also notes, "The earliest preserved Christian art is limited to burial places such as catacombs, to objects like lamps and bowls used in the home, and to rings for the finger. During the first three centuries Christians were able to build only a few places of worship." See Robert Louis Wilken, *The Spirit of Early Christian Thought: Seeking the Face of God* (New Haven, CT: Yale University Press, 2003), 241.

[12] Scripture teaches us that there is one true likeness of God, and that is humankind. Genesis 1:27 explicitly tells us that we are created in the image of God. "Only God can make an image of himself. Man, then, is not to fashion an image of God to worship but rather to worship the God in whose image he is made." See David W. Jones, *An Introduction to Biblical Ethics*, ed. Daniel Heimbach (Nashville: B&H Academic, 2013), 151. There is a wide range of convictions regarding depictions of Jesus, but one thing we can all agree on is that Jesus uniquely fulfilled the second commandment. To see Christ is to see the one true God of the universe, to see the God who could not be seen on Sinai. Jesus is the image (*eikon*) of the invisible God (Col 1:15).

try is related to disordered affections. This idea of disordered affections is of particular interest to our topic. Abraham Kuyper warns his readers, "Beauty makes . . . evil even more alluring, becoming the siren that through its lovely sound seeks to lure us into the depths of destruction."[13] As with any beautiful thing, there is always the risk of luring the recipient to the thing itself rather than serving as a signpost to point others to the God of true beauty.

The Destruction of Idolatrous Images

Second, because of the long history of suspicion toward beauty and aesthetic experience, several theological movements have arisen from the concern that beautiful experiences and images can inadvertently lead believers into idolatry. The most notorious of them, which has reemerged in some form or another throughout church history, is iconoclasm. Iconoclast movements seek to protect the church from idolatry by rejecting and destroying images used in religious contexts—from the whitewashing of paintings in rural churches to the smashing of stained-glass windows in city cathedrals.[14] One notable example is the crisis of the sixteenth-century Protestant Reformation. After Martin Luther made his stand against the doctrines of the medieval Catholic Church at the Diet of Worms, he was whisked into hiding at Wartburg Castle

---

[13] Abraham Kuyper, *Wisdom and Wonder: Common Grace in Science and Art* (Grand Rapids: Christian's Library, 2011), 123.

[14] See Justo Gonzalez, *The Story of Christianity: The Early Church to the Dawn of the Reformation*, vol. 1 (San Francisco: Harper, 1984), 260.

to protect his life.[15] During this time, one of Luther's influential contemporaries, Andreas Bodenstein von Karlstadt, adopted extreme iconoclastic views and began to lead his fellow reformers in destroying stained glass windows, statues, and historical landmarks throughout churches in Wittenberg, Germany. When word came back to Luther of these iconoclast crusades, he came out of hiding at the risk of his own life to stop the movement.

While Martin Luther certainly rejected the Catholic cult of saints, he did not see pictures and statues as dangerous in and of themselves. Before the Reformation, many church leaders utilized icons, statues, and images to teach the faith because many people were illiterate. In contrast, the Reformers argued that people should be taught to read the Bible instead. In this way, people would understand how to worship God as he had revealed himself in the ways he prescribed.[16] But Luther understood that idolatry is a problem with the depraved human heart, not with what we might call beautiful things.[17] As his

---

[15] As the pioneer of the Protestant Reformation, Martin Luther made a stand against the Catholic Church in the early 1500s, taking issue with papal authority, indulgences, their doctrines of justification and works, among other things. Luther, a former priest, sparked the movement from which we now have the Protestant Church. For his defiance, Luther was condemned as a heretic by the Holy Roman emperor Charles V, who placed a generous price on his head.

[16] See the Heidelberg Catechism, Question and Answer 96, https://www.heidelberg-catechism.com/pdf/lords-days/Heidelberg-Catechism.pdf.

[17] As Martin Luther noted, "Whatever your heart clings to . . . that is your God." Large Catechism, The First Commandment, 1529. See Beale, *We Become What We Worship*, 17.

Swiss contemporary John Calvin said, "Man's nature . . . is a perpetual factory of idols."[18] Again, if idolatry is a matter of disproportionate affections, destroying alluring images would not remedy the problem.[19] While the iconoclast movements are on the extreme end of attempts to divert idolatry, theologian Richard Viladesau notes them as "a particular manifestation of a more general problem in Christianity."[20] For many Christians today, beauty retains the ever-present reality of idolatry looming in the shadows. Thus, the shadow of iconoclasm often results in a spirituality that has no tolerance for beauty or aesthetic experience. In one sense, this is understandable because the false seduction of idolatry bids humanity to seek comfort, joy, and hope in things that are unworthy of our worshipful adoration. However, a God-centered vision of beauty will not only displace idolatry but will also position aesthetic experience in its right place so that Christians can benefit from the intentional use of aesthetics in spiritual formation. Furthermore, the

---

[18] John Calvin, *Institutes of the Christian Religion*, ed. John T. McNeill (Philadelphia: Westminster, 1960),

[19] "We only cease to be the slave of one appetite because another taste has brought it into subordination. A youth may cease to idolize sensual pleasure, but it's only because the idol of material gain has gotten the ascendancy. There is not one personal transformation in which the heart is left without an object of ultimate beauty and joy. Its desire for one particular object may be conquered, but its desire to have some object is unconquerable. The only way to dispossess the heart of an old affection is by the expulsive power of a new one." Thomas Chalmers and John Piper, *The Expulsive Power of a New Affection* (Wheaton, IL: Crossway, 2020).

[20] Richard Viladesau, *Theological Aesthetics: God in Imagination, Beauty, and Art* (New York: Oxford University Press, 1999), 52.

proper way to battle idolatry is to go to the foot of the cross, where the worthlessness of idols is exposed by the resplendent glory of God's love.[21]

The Rise of Dualistic Ascetism

Third, our aesthetic malnutrition is also the result of ascetism. Ascetism espouses a lifestyle characterized by abstinence from sensual pleasures, often for the purpose of pursuing spiritual goals. There are many things that we might view as sensory pleasures, yet Scripture demands we avoid them. As Christians, we understand that sinful indulgence, which is abusing or misusing the things of earth, is forbidden. However, there are also many spiritual disciplines, like fasting, where temporary abstinence is practiced as a way to find lasting joy in God. The type of ascetism I am concerned with is the absolute and unqualified prohibition against enjoying the gifts of God within creation. This type of ascetism is most dangerous because it becomes an end in itself, a so-called pathway to spiritual maturity. Consider the self-made religion of the false teachers in Colossae, who exhorted the church to pursue severe treatment of the body with regulations like "Don't handle, don't taste, don't touch" as a means to ascend to a higher level of "wisdom" (Col 2:21–23). In cases like these, the apostle Paul goes so far as to say that those who teach others to treat the God-gifted sensory pleasures of earth legalistically—as unqualifiedly forbidden—are following the teaching of demons (1 Tim 4:1–3).

---

[21] See Kevin J. Vanhoozer, "Praising in Song: Beauty and the Arts," *The Blackwell Companion to Christian Ethics*, ed. Stanley Hauerwas and Samuel Wells (Hoboken, NJ: Wiley-Blackwell, 2004), 110–22.

The historical problem of aesthetic dualism still casts a shadow over contemporary believers because it tends to create a polar dichotomy between the spiritual and physical realms, the immaterial and the material, often to the detriment of the spiritual. As neo-Calvinist Abraham Kuyper rightly observed, the implication of such a dichotomy for beauty and aesthetics tends to "assign beauty to the desires of the flesh, resulting in far less appreciation of beauty and greater inclination to condemn it."[22] However, a holistic biblical worldview would lead us to understand that not all beautiful things and aesthetic experiences are evil in and of themselves. Yet this legalistic dualism gave way to an asceticism that led Christians to be deeply suspicious of the very things in which beauty finds its initial mediation—the body and the senses. For many Christians, the association of aesthetic experience with sensory perceptions and bodily delights pollutes the recipient with an unwelcome worldliness.[23] This leaves many in the church ill-equipped to understand what we might call the proper spiritual trajectory of aesthetic experiences. J. I. Packer writes:

> It is . . . heresy to affirm that the world of matter, physical life, and sensory pleasure is valueless and evil. Down the centuries that heresy has haunted Christian minds and produced many ugly things: a false antithesis between the material and spiritual; false guilt about enjoying food, physical comfort, and sex in marriage; glorification of dirt, seediness, and uncouthness; pride in one's world-denying asceticism; contracting out of

---

[22] Kuyper, *Wisdom and Wonder*, 123.
[23] See Brown, *Religious Aesthetics*, 3.

> the arts and all cultural endeavor ("not spiritual, you know"); and so on. But the truth of the goodness of creation teaches us to negate all such nastiness (for such it really is), and that we must learn to do.[24]

I will argue in later chapters that sensory experience can have a powerful role in the formation of a person from a cognitive, affective, and volitional level.[25] In other words, a proper vision of beauty and aesthetics, as it relates to spiritual formation, could enable us to properly discern and understand the God intended purpose for sensory pleasures. The contemplative view of Christian spirituality may be helpful on this point. Contemplation has to do with a loving attentiveness to God, and it involves all of our faculties—seeing, hearing, tasting, touching, smelling, feeling, and perceiving.[26]

The Deconstruction of the Transcendentals

Fourth, the "transcendentals" of truth, goodness, and beauty have been deconstructed. English philosopher Sir Roger Scruton opens his 2009 documentary, *Why Beauty Matters*, by observing that "at any time between 1750 and 1930 if you had asked educated people to describe the aim of poetry, art or music, they would have

---

[24] J. I. Packer, "The Christian and God's World," in *Serving the People of God: Collected Shorter Writings on The Church, Evangelism, the Charismatic Movement, and Christian Living*, Collected Shorter Writings of J. I. Packer, vol. 2 (Vancouver: Regent College, 1998), 180.

[25] See Evan B. Howard, *The Brazos Introduction to Christian Spirituality* (Grand Rapids: Brazos, 2008), 84–85.

[26] See Glenn Hinson, *Christian Spirituality*, ed. Donald Alexander (Downers Grove, IL: InterVarsity, 1988), 171–87.

replied 'beauty.' And if you had asked for the point of that, you would have learned that beauty is a value—as important as truth and goodness."[27] This is no longer the case. Beauty is no longer an ultimate value. Today, those who are familiar with both religion and philosophy would understand that, from the patristic era to the Enlightenment, this triad of "truth, goodness, and beauty" was understood to be a transcendental group that grounded all human experience in a higher reality. In other words, truth, goodness, and beauty served as the point where eternity permeated creation, being a cemented part of the created order but a continuous presence with the divine. Since beauty was considered a transcendental property of being, it belonged to God's essence.

In the classical Christian tradition, the transcendental nature of truth, goodness, and beauty held that all of these categories found their ultimate source and form in God's nature.[28] For this reason, premodern theologians often utilized this transcendental framework to understand our world as derivative of the divine.[29] As Christian philosopher

---

[27] Roger Scruton, *Why Beauty Matters* (film), 2009, https://www.bing.com/videos/riverview/relatedvideo?q=roger%20scruton%20beauty&mid.

[28] And while the good, true, and beautiful are one, they are also three. Consequently, if the good, true, and beautiful are originally ascribed to God, who is one (Deut 6:4), they cannot be separated or opposed to one another in their inner nature. See Herman Bavinck, *Essays on Religion, Science, and Society* (Grand Rapids: Baker Academic, 2013), 255.

[29] Augustine followed Plato, who understood the good, the beautiful, and the true as being essentially reducible to the same thing. The centrality of beauty in Plato's writings can be found in *Symposium* and the *Dialogues of Phaedrus*. Plato's teacher, Aristotle, has been influential in the field of aesthetics as well, especially in his work *Poetics*.

Garrett J. DeWeese has explained, "The tradition from Plato and Aristotle through Aquinas and the Scholastics regarded the transcendentals as properties of Being, transcending time and place—transcending, that is, the limits of particulars. Consequently, they also transcend personal tastes, cultural values and religious traditions. The transcendentals were proper objects of affection, proper aims of a well-ordered and fulfilled life."[30] Moreover, the unity of the transcendentals was important to the ancients because compartmentalizing these objective realities would, in turn, deconstruct the majesty of the whole. For the ancients, if something was true, it was also good and beautiful. Similarly, for something to be good, it also had to be beautiful and true. For the ancients, beauty disclosed or radiated the truth and goodness of the reality, person, or object being perceived.[31] Thus, the transcendentals are inseparable, and their theological light only shines if undivided.

What happened when the Enlightenment restricted our human experience with a naturalistic, immanent framework? As Vanhoozer argues, "The fate of beauty is tied to that of truth and goodness. What the ancients united, the moderns have differentiated and the postmoderns have deconstructed. Society is still learning to live amidst the ruins."[32] In turn, the divorce of truth, goodness, and beauty left each to become disputed

---

[30] Garrett J. DeWeese, *Doing Philosophy as a Christian*, Christian Worldview Integration Series (Downers Grove, IL: IVP, 2014), 180.

[31] See John Navone, *Toward a Theology of Beauty* (Collegeville, PA: Liturgical, 1996), vii.

[32] Vanhoozer, "Praising in Song," 111.

subjective categories, thus destroying the framework that had long served as the basis for judgments regarding human knowledge and experience. Before these transcendentals ceased to be ultimate values, people lived in what Charles Taylor calls "an enchanted world," open to divine presence and not closed off or self-sufficient.[33] However, this shift in being closed off from the supernatural brought about a disenchantment, a disregarding of any sort of transcendent meaning and significance. Yet we remain haunted by beauty as it points us beyond itself. As James K. A. Smith has aptly observed, "In some fleeting moments of aesthetic enchantment . . . even the secularist is pressed by a sense of something more—some 'fullness' that wells up within (or presses down upon) the immanent frame we've constructed in modernity."[34]

Though the world is still enamored with beauty and enchanted by aesthetic experience, the quest for beauty becomes a fool's errand without truth and goodness. As R. Albert Mohler has observed, the transcendental framework "opens an entirely new awareness for us. We now begin to understand that there is a moral context, a truth context, to every question about beauty. We can no longer talk about beauty as a mere matter of taste. Instantly, by affirming the unity of the transcendentals, we are required to see beauty fundamentally as a matter of truth to which taste is accountable, rather than a matter of taste to which truth is accountable."[35] However,

---

[33] Charles Taylor, *Secular Age* (Cambridge, MA: Belknap, 2018), 25.

[34] James K. A. Smith, *How (Not) to Be Secular: Reading Charles Taylor* (Grand Rapids: Eerdmans, 2014), 12.

[35] Mohler, *The Disappearance of God*, 51.

the transcendentals have now been deconstructed. As a result, beauty turns toward sentimentality, truth toward unattractive historical facts, and goodness toward stale morality.[36] When beauty is turned into sentimentality, we arrive at superficial emotion without proper proportion. However, a Christian understanding of beauty runs counter to the "wisdom" of our age and calls us to reject the modern secular framework and recapture a holistic view of the transcendentals. In returning to the transcendentals, our new vision for the Christian life and our holistic vision for spiritual formation dictate that we must grow in the sound knowledge of God's truth, reflect his goodness in character and action, but also delight in the beautiful triune God. As medieval theologian St. Albert the Great argued, "Beauty is a good that is known and loved in all its truth."[37] In this sense, beauty "clarifies the double focus of theology—on truth and goodness—because it expresses its evidence or even its visible and objective proof."[38]

---

[36] Much of the Christian tradition owes a nod to philosophers for this transcendental framework. However, Bavinck was leery of neo-Platonism in Christian thinking, concerned that the philosophy often overemphasized the limited nature of all earthly manifestations of the good, true, and beautiful. One of the most predominant concerns for Bavinck was the theological fallout of both a too-high and a too-low view of beauty. See Herman Bavinck, "Of Beauty and Aesthetic," in *Essays on Religion, Science and Society*, ed. John Bolt, trans. Harry Boonstra and Gerrit Sheeres (Grand Rapids: Eerdmans, 2008), 255.

[37] See Brendan Thomas Sammon, *Called to Attraction: An Introduction to the Theology of Beauty* (Eugene, OR: Wipf and Stock, 2017), 89–97.

[38] Stephan van Erp, *The Art of Theology: Hans Urs von Balthasar's Theological Aesthetics and Foundations of Faith* (Wilsele, BE: Peeters, 2004), 55.

The Rule of Utilitarianism

Fifth, our consumeristic society values usefulness above all things; and in this context, beauty becomes nothing more than a tertiary benefit, if not a needless distraction. "Getting and spending," says Wordsworth, "we lay waste our powers; / Little we see in nature that is ours; / We have given our hearts away."[39] One of the ways this is most evident, according to Roger Scruton, is in the cult of ugliness that represents much of modern architecture since the industrial revolution. He argues that at the turn of the twentieth century, architects became impatient with beauty and began to put utility in its place.[40] Because of this, our cities are riddled with stale office buildings and brutal concrete compounds that display soullessness and sterility. When form follows function, there is no use for beautiful embellishments or aesthetic ornamentation. However, our society's preference for beautiful buildings over purely utilitarian structures is telling. Often, it's the compounds that are demolished without much opposition, while cathedrals often endure.

There are many areas of modern life where the rise of utilitarianism has resulted in little use for beauty and reflective aesthetic experience. The obsession with functionality has devalued anything that is not "directly useful in mastering the

---

[39] William Wordsworth, "The World Is Too Much with Us," https://www.poetryfoundation.org/poems/45564/the-world-is-too-much-with-us.

[40] Roger Scruton, *Why Beauty Matters* (film), 2009, https://www.bing.com/videos/riverview/relatedvideo?q=roger%20scruton%20beauty&mid.

physical life."[41] The highest goals have become bottom-line efficiency and pragmatic utility. In fact, some people deny that beauty has any role except as an instrument of service to something perceived to be more important.[42] What does one do, in a utilitarian sense, with the euphoric sight of a flowery meadow or the sound of Bedřich Smetana's *The Moldau*? From the perspective of utilitarian pragmatism, many of these aesthetic things in life offer little practical use. God, however, has given beauty and aesthetic experience independently of personal appetites, desires, or utilitarian purposes.

The danger of limiting beauty to its utilitarian value is that it belittles the God of creation and robs humanity of a vast terrain of human exploration and enjoyment.[43] Because of the church's lack of attentiveness to beauty, the potential spiritual enrichment from aesthetics has been lost. Dennis Hollinger notes that "in pragmatic results-oriented cultures we often see aesthetics as superfluous and certainly not related to spirituality . . . in contrast to our quest for results and success. . . . [however, beauty] has a powerful way of sensitizing us to the simple and natural things of life and a way of refreshing our inward selves. Allowing creativity to flourish and seeking aesthetic sensitivity draw us into a sphere of life and spirituality that a purely rational approach cannot achieve."[44] Again, as we will see later, the relationships among beauty, aesthetics, and spiritual formation

---

[41] Leland Ryken, *Culture in Christian Perspective* (Portland, OR: Multnomah, 1986), 74.

[42] See W. David O. Taylor, *For the Beauty of the Church: Casting a Vision for the Arts* (Grand Rapids: Baker, 2010), 153.

[43] See Taylor, 153–54.

[44] Dennis P. Hollinger, *Head, Heart, and Hands* (Downers Grove, IL: IVP, 2005), 134–35.

help Christians see the purpose and benefit of beauty in everyday life. Beauty and aesthetics stir within us a wonder of our world, a needed antidote to the utilitarian world, where we can become too obscured by the mundane and tedious tasks of life, underwhelmed by the ordinary.

The Suspicion toward Natural Theology

Sixth, the reluctance to accept natural theology and general revelation has been detrimental to Christian reflection on beauty, aesthetics, and spiritual formation. Natural theology and general revelation are concerned with the knowledge of God available to all human beings apart from special revelation. Natural theology and general revelation have a long and conspicuous history within Christianity.[45] The influence of Swiss reformed theologian Karl Barth on these subjects has cast a long shadow over modern theology. This shadow adds to the tendency to view natural theology and general revelation with suspicion, as if they are essentially unconnected to special revelation.[46] Barth's views were on the extreme end, arguing that "as the content of proclamation and theology [natural theology] can have no place at all. It can be treated only as non-existent. In this sense, therefore, it must be excised without mercy."[47] For Barth, there was fundamentally no such thing as natural theology. It's

[45] See Millard Erickson, *Christian Theology* (Grand Rapids: Baker Academic, 1998), 180–85.

[46] See Karl Barth, *Church Dogmatics*, ed. G. W. Bromiley and T. F. Torrance (New York: T & T Clark, 2004), II.1, 651. Also, see the discussion between Karl Barth and K. and E. Brunner in Barth and Brunner, *Natural Theology* (London: SCM, 1947).

[47] Karl Barth, *Church Dogmatics*, II.1, 170.

important to understand Barth's context, as his arguments were positioned against a pantheistic drift in Christian theology. Even still, some theologians in the Barthian tradition have all but taken the stance that the denial of natural theology and even general revelation is a central and nonnegotiable position.[48]

Granted, natural theology and general revelation will always hold a secondary place behind special revelation. Barth would go so far as to argue that these realities have no point of contact with the divine. However, as Alister McGrath notes, Barth stands in contrast to the majority of the Christian tradition: "Many Christian writers, from various periods in the history of the church, speak of creation as the 'handiwork of God,' comparing it to a work of art which is both beautiful in itself, as well as expressing the personality of its creator."[49] Lutheran theologians Charles Arand and Erik Herrmann remind us that saints like Irenaeus affirmed the intrinsic goodness of creation. Aquinas celebrated the diversity of God's works in creation as manifestations of God's goodness. And Luther even argues, "If anyone believes them [God's words] and regards them more attentively, he is compelled to wonder at them [the world's beauty], and his wonderment gradually strengthens his faith."[50] In other words, certain knowledge of God is generally available to all people. From the perspective of apologetics, we must grant that God

---

[48] See James Barr, *Biblical Faith and Natural Theology* (New York: Clarendon, 1993), 3–20.

[49] Alister McGrath, *Science & Religion* (Malden, MA: Blackwell, 1999), 117.

[50] See Charles Arand and Erik Herrmann *Attending to the Beauty of Creation and New Creation* in *Scholarly Resources from Concordia Seminary* (April 2019), https://scholar.csl.edu/cgi/=concordiapagesviewcontent.cgi?article=1004&content.

has implanted a sense of the divine in every human being, of which natural theology and general revelation serve as a point of contact for special revelation. Consider the regular operation of natural laws, the fine-tuning of the universe as observed by cosmologists, or the intricacies of living beings and organisms observed by biologists. While this observational knowledge is partial, it does serve as evidence of a divine Creator behind the natural world.

In turn, most theologians would grant that "God has given us objective, valid, rational revelation of himself in nature, history, and human personality."[51] Without understanding the benefit of natural revelation, Christians lose a sense of the greatness of God and even his love for them expressed in the goodness of creation. General revelation and the natural world can be powerful portals through which humans experience God's glory. Moreover, personal experiences with the beauty of creation can evoke a tangible longing for God. These experiences can also be harnessed to direct the spiritually formative practices of the church.

Conclusion

In the 2005 commencement speech to the graduating class at Kenyon College, American novelist David Foster Wallace told the story of two young fish meeting an older fish who was swimming along in the opposite direction. As the older fish passed by, he nodded at them and said, "Morning, boys. How's the water?" The two young fish continued on their way, and

---

[51] Millard Erickson, *Christian Theology* (Grand Rapids: Baker Academic, 1998), 194.

eventually one looked over at the other and asked, "What is water?"[52] The point being, fish do not know they are in water. Too often, it is hardest to see the most obvious and ubiquitous realities that shape our understanding and "being" in the world. In this chapter, I have described the intellectual stream you are most likely swimming in or against. In many ways, being a "fish out of water" helps us understand how a distinctly Christian vision of the world—and thus, beauty and aesthetics—not only situates us within God's created order rightly but also calls us to see more clearly. We do not have to accept the false dichotomy between the mystical and monastic life when it comes to aesthetics. We do not have to understand beauty as either vain extravagance or reject it for drab functionality. It's time to come up for air. While the observations offered in this chapter should give cause for concern, all hope is not lost for the church's use of beauty and aesthetics for spiritual formation. As Edward Farley aptly notes, "To be a beast, beauty must at least be noticed in order to be feared or refuted."[53]

---

[52] This speech by David Foster Wallace was eventually turned into a little book titled *This Is Water: Some Thoughts, Delivered on a Significant Occasion, about Living a Compassionate Life* (New York: Little, Brown, 2009).

[53] Edward Farley, *Faith and Beauty: A Theological Aesthetic* (Burlington, VT: Ashgate, 2001), 5–6.

3

The World, the Word, and Wide-Eyed Wonder

Beauty and the Two Books of God

At times my heart cries out with longing to see. . . . If I can get so much pleasure from mere touch, how much more beauty must be revealed by sight. Yet, those who have eyes apparently see little. The panorama of color and action which fills the world is taken for granted. It is human, perhaps, to appreciate little that which we have and to long for that which we have not, but it is a great pity that in the world of light the gift of sight is used only as a mere convenience rather than as a means of adding fullness to life.

—*Helen Keller, "Three Days to See,"* Atlantic Monthly

When Beauty Breaks Forth

The restaurant hostess navigated Ruth, Charles, and Thomas through the crowded dining room to a table nestled in the most secluded spot in the restaurant. The table alcove was enclosed by floor-to-ceiling windows that early nineteenth-century carpenters had framed in mahogany wood, windows that provided a breathtaking view of the snow-capped mountains of this British Columbia village. It was the most suitable setting for the reflective conversations the three friends had come to cherish. Over the years, the three former graduate school companions had met here annually to ski, catch up, and discuss their most recent interests and academic ventures. Thomas, an agnostic philosophy professor, enjoyed exploring the existential questions concerning the meaning of life. Ruth, an atheist sociologist, was most eager to hear the opinions of Charles and Thomas on the ways that humans could empower others to flourish for the good of local communities. While Charles, the naturalist and laboratory researcher, relished the opportunity to share the latest findings of the scientific community. As their conversation meandered into the late hours of the afternoon, the entire restaurant seemed to quiet down in the solemn instant of the sun settling into the horizon. In that moment, the remaining light cascaded across the edges of the pure white snow, and the once blue sky seemed as if it was burning away with a fluorescent orange glow. Charles broke the silence: "Isn't this stunning!" Thomas calmly approved with an exhaled, "Absolutely beautiful." Ruth, in wide-eyed wonder, held out her glass to toast the occasion of their momentary mutual experience.

There is a whisper of familiarity in the awe captured in this scene, isn't there? It is not difficult to imagine ourselves among these three friends raising our own glass. For these three friends, as with many people, these types of aesthetically rich experiences tend to move our hearts into the realm of religious affection and philosophical reflection. Humanity apprehends reality truly, even if subjectively, and each of us does so with varying degrees of accuracy. But if we as Christians dared to press in on the intellectual commitments of the three secular intellectuals at the table, we would be met with a certain amount of tension. From the perspective of a Christian, if an agnostic, atheist, and naturalist were to discuss the ultimate purpose and meaning of their shared experience, they would ultimately falter and fall short. You see, the naturalist scientist may be able to explain *how* the twilight sun ignites the sky with warm hues of orange and red. But apart from divine revelation, the naturalist cannot explain *why* this beautiful phenomenon exists. The agnostic philosopher may be able to journey through the history of pontifications given by the world's greatest thinkers on the subject of beauty. But apart from God's revealed Word, the philosopher cannot definitively state the ultimate *purpose* of beauty. The atheist sociologist may be able to explain why these common aesthetic experiences are treasured among fellow humans. But apart from understanding God's purposes in creation, the sociologist cannot explain *what* the experience of beauty is meant to point humanity toward.

The secular philosopher, sociologist, and scientist would find that as they conquered the highest peak of natural knowledge and pulled themselves over the final rock, they would be, as Robert Jastrow puts it, "greeted by a band of theologians who have been sitting there for centuries."[1] The reason is simple. One of the distinct contributions of Christian theology in the discussion of beauty and aesthetics is found in the belief that God reveals what the secular humanitarian sciences cannot, namely, that such encounters point beyond the beauty of creation itself to something (Someone) higher. While all would hold that beauty and aesthetic experiences communicate something, as Christians have long believed, our theology offers the most compelling interpretation of what is being communicated on the canvas of creation.

The Two Books of God: General and Special Revelation

One must begin the study of beauty and aesthetics the same way all subjects of inquiry from a uniquely Christian perspective begin, namely, with the doctrine of revelation. The doctrine of revelation stands apart as the fundamental epistemological axiom of Christianity and is the theological foundation for the exploration of beauty and aesthetics. Christianity is, after all, a revealed religion. The Christian doctrine of revelation is concerned with the study of how, when, and where God reveals his presence, nature, and actions. Fundamentally, Christians have long held that God alone "circumscribes and determines what can be known."[2] Thus, Christian theology must begin with revelation because humans alone cannot think rightly

---

[1] Robert Jastrow, *God of the Astronomers*, 2nd ed. (New York: Norton, 1992), 107.

[2] Gregory Alan Thornbury, *Recovering Classical Evangelicalism: Applying the Wisdom and Vision of Carl F. H. Henry* (Wheaton, IL: Crossway, 2013), 52–53.

about the world or anything in it apart from God's disclosure. Consequently, any encounter with beauty comes from an act of intentional, self-revealing love on the part of God. From the very outset, then, the doctrine of revelation teaches us that God is the source of beauty and that humanity's preoccupation with beauty and any pure aesthetic experience is God ordained.

Two distinctions have been traditionally applied to the doctrine of revelation. These two distinctions have sometimes been called the "two books of God" and are further designated as general and special revelation.[3] While Scripture does not explicitly distinguish between general and special revelation, the distinction helps us understand the teleological difference between the two in their essential nature, comprehensiveness, and served purpose in relation to beauty.[4] Following the prescribed order of these two books of creation, let's begin with the first book: general revelation.

General Revelation

In an effort to bring the doctrine of general revelation into focus in accordance with the teachings of Scripture, we must explore creational theology. The terms *general revelation*, *common grace*, and *natural theology* are related and often used in this area of study. However, the term *creational theology* can help avoid much of the culturally conditioned confusion, and it underscores the foundational belief that we are discussing the

[3] John H. Gerstner, *Christian Faith and Modern Theology*, ed. Carl F. H. Henry (New York: Channel Press, 1964), 97.

[4] See Louis Berkhof, *Systematic Theology* (Carlisle, PA: Banner of Truth Trust, 2021), 126.

creation of God.[5] The primary task of creational theology is to help us read the pages of the "book of the world."[6] Creational theology engages the aesthetic experiences of the world's beauty through a distinctly Christian vision, "with the conviction that the resources of the Christian worldview will enable better understanding . . . as well as deepen them."[7]

The Book of the World: The Beauty of the World

Within the Christian tradition, we find that the beauty of the created world is a gift of grace from God to enrich our experience and ultimately point us back to him. To put it plainly, the beauty of our world inevitably carries with it a sense of God's nearness. Centuries ago, in a letter to the Christians in Rome, the apostle Paul taught us that what can be known about God is evident because God has chosen to make it known: "What can be known about God is evident among them, because God has shown it to them. For his invisible attributes, that is, his eternal power and divine nature, have been clearly seen since the creation of the world, being understood through what he has made. As a result, people are without excuse" (Rom 1:19–20).

Paul's choice of wording in Rom 1:20 is worth further consideration because God is understood through what is created or made. What has been translated in English Bibles as "what

---

[5] See T. M. Moore, *Consider the Lilies: A Plea for Creational Theology* (Eugene, OR: Pickwick, 2014); or L. Clifton Edwards's *Creation's Beauty as Revelation: Toward a Creational Theology of Natural Beauty* (Eugene, OR: Wipf and Stock, 2014).

[6] Moore, *Consider the Lilies*, 65.

[7] Edwards, *Creation's Beauty as Revelation,* xiv.

has been made" is taken from a composite Greek word that has the same linguistic origins as our word *poem*. It's a curious choice of words for Paul because it is rarely used in the New Testament.[8] The concept seems to illuminate the idea that the beautiful universe and everything in it is God's poetic work of art.[9] Just as a moving poem points the reader to the creative gifts of the author, so too through general revelation has God made his existence evident to all mankind with his beautiful creative work in the universe. While beauty communicates nonverbally, it functions like poetry in that it facilitates pause and reflection in the recipient.[10] In this sense, creation takes on the character of art, in which beauty reveals the undeniable presence of God apart from words. Moreover, because creation is general revelation, this appreciation of beauty is understood across cultures and various religions. Thus, God has disclosed his infinite and transcendent beauty in a general way to be experienced by all in creation.[11] As Paul demonstrated, we are accountable for that revelation because we are without excuse.

Indeed, the first chapters of Genesis portray that from the inception of creation, the infinite God poured himself

---

[8] Ποιήμασιν (*poiēmasin*) comes from the root word ποίημα (*poiēma*). The word only appears in the Greek New Testament twice in reference to "workmanship" or something that has been "made" (Rom 1:20; Eph 2:10). We will consider the other use of this word in the New Testament in a later chapter.

[9] Augustine also spoke of God revealing himself in the "divine art" of creation. See Augustine, *The Trinity*, trans. Stephen McKenna, vol. 45 of The Fathers of the Church series (Washington, DC: Catholic University of America Press, 1963), 6.12 (p. 214).

[10] See Edwards, *Creation's Beauty as Revelation*, 84.

[11] See C. John Collins, *Science and Faith: Friends or Foes?* (Wheaton, IL: Crossway, 2003), 181.

intimately into the poetic work of his finite creation. Creation is a beautiful work of art as well as an expression of the beauty of its Creator. The image of God as artist is profoundly helpful when thinking about God creating our cosmic something "out of nothing," analogous to an author who imagines and then pens an epic novel or a composer who writes and conducts a symphony.[12] Thus, Genesis presents God as an artist, making things "intelligently and freely, for his own delight."[13] As Paul Evdokimov eloquently proclaims, the first day of creation is a joyous hymn sung by God himself, and the flashing eruption of "Let there be light" (Gen 1:3) means "let the revelation be," a calling forth from the formless void.[14] The creation account of Genesis affirms God's pleasure in his handiwork by declaring each act as "good" seven times, denoting—among other things—that what has been created is delightful and pleasant, and doing so by employing aesthetic terms (Gen 1:31). The use of this "good" declaration in the context of original creation hints at the aesthetic nature of God's evaluative judgment upon the things he has made. This is picked up by many of the biblical writers who often describe the elements of creation—from lands to trees and even stones—as beautiful and pleasant as well (Gen 2:9; 3:6; Ps 48:2; 50:2; 104:16; Isa 60:13; Jer 3:19; Ezek 27:3–4; 31:7–8; Dan 11:16; Hos 14:6; Zech 4:7; Luke 21:5).

---

[12] This analogy is from Dorothy Sayers, *Mind of the Maker* (San Francisco: Harper, 1987).

[13] John-Mark L. Miravalle, *Beauty: What It Is and Why It Matters* (Manchester, NH: Sophia Institute, 2019), 20.

[14] Paul Evdokimov, *The Art of the Icon: A Theology of Beauty*, trans. Fr. Steven Bigham (Torrance, CA: Oakwood, 1990), 6–7.

It is proper, therefore, that we as Christians nurture delight in this universe of wonders in which we reside. God has created the world to be primed with opportunities for such enchantment, experiences that can be harnessed to aid us in coming to our theological senses. For this reason, the beauties of creation are a vast territory for exploration. The natural world has long been held as a stimulus of theology in that it is "God's imprint of Himself through the created order of things."[15] However, while Christian theologians have long held that the knowledge of God is accessible through general revelation, it is generally understood that such knowledge is limited in "scope, in coherence, and in depth."[16] In other words, general revelation of creation does not provide the key to its own existence. General revelation, then, is "not so much a 'source' for theology as it is an inspiration for theology" or as a "significant analogy to the creator of all."[17]

What, Then, Is the World For?

Perhaps you have seen Frank Darabont's critically acclaimed film, *The Shawshank Redemption*, which tells the story of banker Andy Dufresne, who despite his claims of innocence, is sentenced to life in Shawshank State Penitentiary for the

---

[15] Michael Bird, *Evangelical Theology: A Biblical and Systematic Introduction* (Grand Rapids: Zondervan Academic, 2020), 70.

[16] Alister E. McGrath, *Christian Theology: An Introduction* (West Sussex, UK: Blackwell, 2011), 152.

[17] Bird, *Evangelical Theology,* 72, and John Frame, *Systematic Theology: An Introduction to Christian Belief* (Eugene, OR: P&R, 2013), 253.

murders of his wife and her lover. In one of the most powerful scenes of the film, the viewer accompanies Andy as he cleans out the prison warden's office. While cleaning, he comes across a stack of vinyl records and plays a beautiful soprano duet from Mozart's *The Marriage of Figaro*. As the song plays, Andy turns on the intercom system so that the music circulates throughout the entire prison yard. Andy's good friend "Red," played by Morgan Freeman, remarks what happens in this moment with voice-over narration:

> I have no idea to this day what those two Italian ladies were singing about. I'd like to think they were singing about something so beautiful it can't be expressed in words, and it makes your heart ache because of it. I tell you those voices soared, higher and farther than anybody in a grey place dares to dream. It was like some beautiful bird flapped into our drab little cage and made these walls dissolve away, and for the briefest of moments, every last man in Shawshank felt free.[18]

In that one brief moment, the condemned men of Shawshank all stood still in silence as the beauty of that song broke forth like rays of warm light into their cold and dark existence. And still, as Red remarks, it would be wonderful to know what precisely the opera duet was about. Christians often feel the same way about beauty in creation. What is it singing about? Can anyone translate creation's nonverbal communication?

---

[18] Frank Darabont, dir., *The Shawshank Redemption* (film), 1994.

Special Revelation: The Beauty of the Word

As Christians, we understand how the limitations of general revelation expose the need for our second book, special revelation. The good news is, God is not silent. God's revealed Word, the Bible, plays a distinct clarifying role in understanding the beauty of the world. Providing lucidity to the manner in which God has made himself known, the psalmist writes in Ps 19:1–4a:

> The heavens declare the glory of God,
> and the expanse proclaims the work of his hands.
> Day after day they pour out speech;
> night after night they communicate knowledge.
> There is no speech; there are no words;
> their voice is not heard.[19]
> Their message has gone out to the whole earth,
> and their words to the ends of the world.

If you've ever sat under a clear night sky, taking in the vast glowing constellations piercing the darkness, it is not difficult to imagine David, who spent much of his early years under the majestic Palestinian sky as a shepherd, pondering the breathtaking artistry of our God. Notice that in Psalm 19, David proclaims that the heavens pour out, like the perpetual bubbling of a spring, a divine declaration of God's glory. The heavens, the

---

[19] One might ask, "How do the skies speak if they have no words?" Or "How do the stars communicate if they have no voice?" This psalm is poetic in nature, so we can understand that David is using personification. In the same way, I might say an instrumental music piece or painting "speaks to me." While these pieces have no words, they speak to us in the deeper aesthetic dimensions of perception.

stars themselves, proclaim the glory of God! The world, that most eloquent book of creation, serves its revelatory function, not in words or propositions but in images and symbols.

Being nonverbal in character, these aesthetic experiences are only limitedly describable. Without special revelation, in this case Psalm 19, we would not know that the purpose of the heaven's beautiful stars (general revelation) is to point back to the one true creator God. In this sense, Scripture and creation interpenetrate one another and confirm one another's testimony. Note that there is an interesting shift in the language of Psalm 19 as you move from v. 1, where David uses a general word for "God," to vv. 7 and on, where David begins using the covenant name of God, Yahweh, rendered as "LORD" in the CSB and many other Bible translations. Thus, while the beginning of Psalm 19 introduces the visible way in which all people are introduced to the invisible God, the later verses give our God's personal name. The implication is that God's Word (special revelation) is more intimate and personal than the general work of creation. Gregory of Nyssa captures the movement of this psalm well: "Admiration even of the beauty of the heavens, and of the dazzling sunbeams, and, indeed, of any fair phenomenon, will then cease. The beauty noticed there will be but as the hand to lead us to the love of the supernal Beauty whose glory the heavens and the firmament declare, and whose secret the whole creation sings."[20]

Gregory reminds us that the beauty of the created world is meant to be a signpost pointing beyond itself to the Creator of

[20] Saint Gregory of Nyssa, *On Virginity*, trans. William Moore; ed. D. P. Curtin (Philadelphia: Dalcassian, 2018), 29.

all, the one true God of the universe, and it is a message that goes out to the ends of the earth.

The World, the Word, and Spiritual Formation

As we have seen, Christians believe that revelation is an act of intentional, self-revealing love on the part of God. If the beauty of the world holds within it a suggestion of the divine, the question of God's intent in creation should be the proper focus of any exploration of aesthetic experiences. Christian theology teaches us that our aesthetic experience is only secondary to God's purpose in glorifying himself. Thus, beauty is a gift of grace because it points us back to him. As Sam Storms has said, "Divine beauty is absolute, unqualified, and independent. All created reality, precisely because it is derivative of the Creator, is beautiful in a secondary sense and only to the degree that it reflects the excellencies of God and fulfills the purpose for which He has made it."[21]

Not only do these transcendent experiences of beauty draw us out from ourselves and allow us to bask in the splendor of God's creative hand; they also have a formative function in our spiritual lives as well. Cultivating a creational theology encourages enchantment with God's handiwork. As we see in Psalm 104, there is a proper response of awe when one considers that God has chosen to enrich our lives by disclosing his power through breathtaking beauty and delightful aesthetic experiences. God did not have to show us the warm colors

---

[21] Sam Storms, "One Thing: Developing a Passion for the Beauty of God," *Christian Focus* (2004): 53–54.

of fall leaves spanning across the horizon of the Appalachian Mountains. God was not required to disclose his sweet benevolence in the greens and yellows of a sunflower field. It is no coincidence that we can enjoy the robin's morning song as it carries through our windows at the break of each day. One must remember, as Calvin Seerveld wrote, that beautiful things and aesthetic experience are "the rainbows God made for a fallen world."[22]

As creation exults in the artistry of the Creator, we must understand that we are intended to enjoy the enriching experiences that God has so lovingly laid before us. This requires a certain amount of spongelike receptivity as the beauty of creation continually washes over and through us, and we as his creatures must be attuned to what is "being said in many senses."[23] For this reason, we must position ourselves to be intentionally mindful of such beauty as we encounter it in a world that is "charged with the grandeur of God."[24] The vast riches of these aesthetic experiences are far too great to be neglected or ignored, for they are God's infinite and transcendent beauty breaking forth in a general way to be enjoyed in creation order, a gift of grace. Creation, then, is not an impersonal system. After all, our personal God has saturated creation with beauty in such a way that we should be astonished in awe. And this strike of wonder at

---

[22] Calvin Seerveld, *Rainbows for the Fallen World: Aesthetic Life and Artistic Task* (Toronto: Tuppence, 2005), 8.

[23] William Desmond, *The Voiding of Being: The Doing and Undoing of Metaphysics in Modernity* (Washington, DC: Catholic University of America Press, 2020), 2.

[24] Gerard Manley Hopkins, "God's Grandeur," in Bernard W. Kelly, *The Mind and Poetry of Gerard Manley Hopkins* (New York: Haskell House, 1971), 5.

the aesthetic richness of the world awakens us from what has so often become modernity's bone-dry rationalism.

As Christians, we must acknowledge that aesthetic delight can provide a significant bridge between human experience and Christian theology. Returning to our fictional anecdote of the three secular friends at the beginning of this chapter, it is noticeable that their appreciation of beauty assumes some sort of objective framework of mutual satisfaction. In general, all humans voice certain affections that accompany aesthetic experiences, often described with words such as *delight*, *awe*, or *reverence*. In this sense, captivation with beauty is our God-given orientation to our Creator, whether we recognize this connection explicitly or not.[25] Thus, we can argue that the beauty of creation is a powerful tool in bolstering our own faith, as well as providing a distinctly Christian apologetic witness. According to Balthasar, even the skeptic would never "come to affirm the truth of revelation unless" he or she "first perceive[d] it as beautiful."[26] After all, Christians hold to the belief that Scripture puts forth the most compelling interpretation of our world. Indeed, Christianity presents a specific view about our world; "and if that view is true, if the world is the way our faith says it is, then a life that does not correspond to Christianity is a life that does not correspond to reality."[27] For the Christian,

---

[25] See Richard Viladesau, *Theology and the Arts: Encountering God Through Music, Art and Rhetoric* (Mahwah, NJ: Paulist, 2000), 42; David Bentley Hart, *The Beauty of the Infinite: The Aesthetics of Christian Truth* (Grand Rapids: Eerdmans, 2003), 17.

[26] Edward T. Oakes, S.J., *The Beauty of God,* ed. Daniel J. Treier, Mark Husbands, and Roger Lundin (Downers Grove, IL: IVP Academic 2007), 212.

[27] Miravalle, *Beauty*, 42.

the natural world is not at all just "natural." As C. S. Lewis once observed, beauty is like "news from a country we have never yet visited."[28] Perhaps the experience of beauty is a dimly inherited memory of Eden.

Conclusion

Not too long ago, I was on a midmorning walk with our youngest daughter through the park that sits adjacent to our neighborhood. There is a section of the winding trails that takes you downhill and eventually spills out into an open meadow with a small pond surrounded by grand oak trees. As we approached the pond, she wanted to sit on the park bench to rest her little legs. As we were enjoying our respite in the warmth of the sun's rays, a breeze swooped through the meadow and began rustling the leaves in the trees. She noticed the sunlight dancing across the ripples in the water and pointed out the synchronized dance of the tall blades of grass. I simply said, "God made all of this to remind you of his goodness," to which she smiled. Her smile I understood as her delightful profession in response to creation's profession. As Jonathan Edwards once said, "When we are delighted with flowery meadows and gentle breezes of wind, we may consider that we only see the emanations of the sweet benevolence of Jesus Christ."[29] Indeed, God "adorns the insects and flowers of the field with

---

[28] C. S. Lewis, *The Weight of Glory* (San Francisco: Harper, 2001), 13.

[29] Jonathan Edwards, *The Works of Jonathan Edwards*, vol. 13, *The "Miscellanies," a–500*, ed. Thomas A. Schafer (New Haven, CT: Yale University Press, 1994), 278–80.

a beauty and elegance far beyond all that can be found in the courts of kings."[30]

This brief exchange with my daughter reminded me of the power of the childlike wonder that sees our world as enchanted with reminders of God's sweet benevolence. Every awe-filled sight, melodic sound, and delightful smell blossoms with deeper meaning when experienced through senses awakened by his Spirit. We only need to be attentive, that is, to tune our hearts and train our imagination to see. Phillip Keller says:

> Whenever I am afield or outdoors, there steals over me the acute consciousness that I am confronted on every hand by the superb workmanship of my Father. It is as if every tree, rock, river, flower, mountain, bird, or blade of grass had stamped upon it the indelible label, "Made by God." Is it any wonder that in a simple yet sublime sense of devotion, respect, and reverence for all life, Christ longed for His Father's name to be hallowed throughout the earth?[31]

God has provided an infinite horizon of natural experience, both celestial and terrestrial. Our call to perpetually seek the beauty around us does not mean we should ever fear exhausting it. Because it has its source in the infinite God, beauty is inexhaustible.[32] It does not matter if your "sense appetites" are as

---

[30] Quoted in Philip Graham Ryken, *Beauty Is Your Destiny: How the Promise of Splendor Changes Everything* (Wheaton, IL: Crossway, 2023), 47.

[31] W. Phillip Keller, *A Layman Looks at the Lord's Prayer* (Chicago: Moody, 2017).

[32] Benjamin P. Myers, *A Poetics of Orthodoxy: Christian Truth as Aesthetic Foundation* (Eugene, OR: Wipf and Stock, 2020), 70.

undeveloped as a child's or as sophisticated as that of a scholar. All things in creation were made according to the infinite mind of the Creator, and the depths of his brilliance can never be fully appreciated or exhausted by finite intelligence. When beauty calls, we are innately created to respond in the hope of continuing the dialogue. In this sense, all people are predisposed to contemplate God through their experience of beauty in the world. We might argue that beauty itself prompts a tacitly religious experience. We are accountable for that revelation. Its knowledge is rooted in our mind-body competencies or instincts of the world.

Scripture alone clarifies the *telos* (ultimate purpose) of these experiences and aids in cultivating our theological senses. It is the Christian's duty then, as Eccl 1:13 says, to apply our minds to examine and explore through wisdom all that is done under heaven. As the psalmist says, "The LORD's works are great, studied by all who delight in them" (Ps 111:2). Or as Barnabas and Paul proclaimed to their listeners in Lystra, "We are proclaiming good news to you, that you turn from these worthless things to the living God, who made the heaven, the earth, the sea, and everything in them. . . . He did not leave himself without a witness, since he did what is good by giving you rain from heaven and fruitful seasons and filling you with food and your hearts with joy" (Acts 14:15–17). It should not be lost on us that God's self-revelation in creation is a conscious, voluntary, and intentional act of love on our behalf. As Carl F. H. Henry observed, this divinely initiated communitive act is by sheer grace in which God alone turns his personal privacy into a deliberately public disclosure of himself.[33]

[33] Carl F. H. Henry, *God, Revelation and Authority*, vol. 2, *God Who Speaks and Shows, Fifteen Theses*, Part 1 (Wheaton, IL: Crossway, 1999), 28.

The pleasure of God is found in enjoying the delightful sights, sounds, and smells of his creation. Their intricate design, harmony, and decorativeness testify "to the skill of the divine artist" and are "proof that God is indeed [creation's] Maker."[34] Creation is a map that leads back to him, after all, because "roses wilt, redwoods tumble, sunsets fade, but God remains."[35]

---

[34] Marsilio Ficino, quoted in Patrick Sherry, *Spirit and Beauty: An Introduction to Theological Aesthetics* (London: SCM, 2002), 3.

[35] Amanda Jenkins, "Theology Thursday: Finding Beauty in All of Life," Grand Canyon University blog, October 21, 2021, https://www.gcu.edu/blog/theology-ministry/theology-thursday-finding-beauty-all-life.

4

Behold, Our Beautiful God

Tasting and Seeing That the Lord Is Good

> [God] acts as the One who gives pleasure, creates desire and rewards with enjoyment, because he is the one who is pleasant, desirable, full of enjoyment, because first and last He alone is that which is pleasant, desirable, and full of enjoyment. God loves us as the One who is worthy of love as God. This is what we mean when we say God is beautiful.
>
> —*Karl Barth,* Church Dogmatics

The Beautiful God Who Is Worthy of Worship

Imagine that you are attending the opening night of a renowned painter's exhibition in a prestigious art gallery. The space is filled with ambient noise as you and the other attendees mingle and admire the displayed paintings. The room is teeming with enjoyment, until the artist abruptly interrupts the conversations to disclose his identity to the attendees and, in doing so, demands praise and excessive adulation: "I have come tonight to receive your worship. By me and me alone have these paintings been brought into reality! For I and I alone deserve your undisputed admiration! I am the artist, and I will not give my glory to another."

The once chatter-filled room is now replaced with awkward silence. Everyone is speechless at the artist's delusional and desperate display of megalomania. After all, anyone with the slightest sense of social sensibility would find this artist's self-exalting requests repulsive and disagreeable, right? How, then, does one deal with the God of the Bible, who demands unadulterated praise from all in creation? Remember Psalm 19? "The heavens declare the glory of God." As you might have noticed, the last sentence in the fictional artist's declaration is a play on Isa 42:8, which reads "I am the LORD. That is my name, and I will not give my glory to another." Is God, then, a megalomaniac? Perhaps this is the perception of those who have not been graced with spiritual eyes to see. However, as Christians, we would understand that the essential difference between the artist in the gallery and the omnipotent Creator of the universe is infinite. One does not need to be a trained psychologist to understand that the demand of worship issued by the fictional gallery artist arises from a desperate self-centered need to fill his own deficiencies.

Contrary to our fictional artist, Christians have long affirmed that God is perfect, that is, without deficiencies (Ps 18:30; 19:7; Matt 5:48). By this we mean that, unlike all other beings, God lacks no desirable attributes or qualities in himself. While God's perfection is often defined negatively, he is without deficiency.

Beauty advances our vision of God positively in that he possesses all desirable attributes or qualities in himself. Even more, God does not merely possess attributes; he is. Therefore, God desires worship not because it meets *his* need but because it meets *our* need.[1] The apostle Paul is emphatic on this point: God is not worshiped by us "as though he needed anything" (Acts 17:25), because he is perfect in himself.[2] The demand for worship from our sovereign God is therefore issued out of his generous love in sharing his inner-trinitarian life, in which there are no deficiencies. Jonathan Edwards argued as much when saying, "There is an infinite fullness of all possible good in God, a fullness of every perfection, of all excellency and beauty, and of infinite happiness."[3]

Now, in regard to God's beauty, the psalmist attests, "From Zion, the perfection of beauty, God appears in radiance" (Ps 50:2). If, as the psalmist declares, God is the perfection of beauty, then his beauty must be greater than anything that can be conceived.[4] It would stand to reason, then, that God is

---

[1] See "Is God a Megalomaniac?," *Desiring God*, audio transcript from *Ask Pastor John* podcast, episode 1111, October 25, 2017, https://www.desiringgod.org/interviews/is-god-a-megalomaniac.

[2] See John M. Frame, *Doctrine of God* (Phillipsburg, NJ: P&R, 2002), 606.

[3] Jonathan Edwards, "Miscellany # 293," in *The Works of Jonathan Edwards*, vol. 13, *The "Miscellanies," a–500*, ed. Thomas A. Schafer (New Haven, CT: Yale University Press, 1994), 384; *The Dissertation Concerning the End for Which God Created the World* 8, 432–33. See also John Carrick, *Jonathan Edwards and the Immediacy of God* (Eugene, OR: Wipf and Stock, 2020), 40.

[4] See Anselm's ontological argument in *Proslogion*, pp. 82–104, in St. Anselm, *Anselm of Canterbury: The Major Works*, Oxford World's Classics, ed. Brian Davies and G. R. Evans, reissue ed. (Oxford, UK: Oxford University Press, 2008), 82–104.

the only being in the universe for whom self-exaltation is justifiable because he alone embodies perfection of beauty (Ps 92:1; 95:6; 103:1) In other words, God's beauty is archetypal beauty. That is, beauty is carried to its highest perfection in him. All other beauties are only by virtue of derivation, participating in and imitating God's beauty in some way. To use the language of the transcendentals, in God's nature we find the highest good, the highest truth, and the highest beauty (Ps 27:4; 119:68; John 14:16). In *The Nature of True Virtue*, Jonathan Edwards claims that God is "the foundation and fountain of all being and all beauty . . . of whom, and through whom, and to whom is all being and all perfection; and whose being and beauty are, as it were, the sum of comprehension of all existence and excellence."[5]

From God's perfection, we would also affirm that he is absolutely undivided and indivisible—unlike things in creation, which are composed in parts. Consider the beauty of God as compared to any created being we might find beautiful. Take, for example, a celebrity who is widely regarded for being physically attractive. While being regarded "beautiful," he or she might also have an irreparably tarnished reputation because of a lack of moral character. Indeed, take into consideration all the attributes of any being other than God, and that person would fall woefully short of perfection and, thus, be unqualified to receive praise. In theology, we often examine God's attributes in parts, but it is important to keep in mind that our God is one. We might think of God's attributes as the lines, colors,

---

[5] Jonathan Edwards, *The Nature of True Virtue*, ed. Matthew Stanley (Ann Arbor: University of Michigan Press, 1960), 15.

shapes, and textures in a painting, which are in proportionate relationship and interplay with one another to depict the whole. Or consider Roger Scruton's analogy of music for our understanding of God's oneness: "In music, all distance between movements is abolished. . . . No musical element excludes any other, but all coexist in a placeless self-presentation. . . . It is as though these many currents flowed together in a single life, at one with itself."[6]

When listening to music, we intuitively understand that we only ever hear songs as a whole, that is, one piece communicated through the diverse sounds. Similarly, because our God is one, perfect and indivisible, there is no variation or shadow of turning in him (Jas 1:17–18). Therefore, when we consider all the attributes of God together without distinction, we can conclude that the pure blazing beauty of God is the radiance of his glorious nature (1 Chron 16:29; 2 Chron 20:21; Ps 29:2).[7] Beauty, then, has a gathering power because it is the resplendence of all God's attributes. Beauty is related to glory in this sense, as glory refers to the consummate beauty of the totality of his perfections.

The Beautiful God Who Reveals Himself

From here we could press further and argue that God is not only the origin of beauty but is also the benevolent giver of all

---

[6] Roger Scruton, *The Aesthetics of Music* (Oxford, UK: Clarendon, 1997), 338–39.

[7] See Raymond C. Ortlund Jr., *Isaiah: God Saves Sinners*, ed. R. Kent Hughes (Wheaton, IL: Crossway, 2005), 237.

aesthetic delights. If God is the foundation and fountain of all being and all beauty, then all beauty must find its origin in him and break forth from him.[8] We would deduce this from Scripture, as we are told that God is the "wellspring of life" (Ps 36:9), for "from him and through him and to him are all things" (Rom 11:36). Indeed, if beauty is primarily found in the realm of the theological, then our journey toward beauty must not only start with God but also delve into the metaphysical, that is, toward origins and first principles.[9]

Thus, to address the ultimate questions of all meaning in beauty, we look to the foundation of all metaphysics in Gen 1:1: "In the beginning God created the heavens and the earth." As the first words of Scripture proclaim, God is and has always been. In front of time itself, before the beginning, God has always existed. Not only has God always existed, but he has always existed independent of anything or anyone else. This means that our triune God is self-existent and self-sufficient in himself and has freely chosen to create the universe and everything therein. Therefore, if Gen 1:1 is taken as a whole, we come to see that all things that exist in the universe are derivative of God; they exist in relation to God.[10] Thus, God is

---

[8] See Jonathan Edwards, *The Nature of True Virtue: A Jonathan Edwards Reader*, ed. John E. Smith, Harry S. Stout, and Kenneth P. Minkema (London: Yale University Press, 1995), 252–53.

[9] See Joseph D. Wooddell, *The Beauty of the Faith* (Eugene, OR: Wipf and Stock, 2010), 47.

[10] Jonathan Edwards wrote, "God is God, and distinguished from all other beings, exalted above 'em, chiefly by his divine beauty, which is infinitely diverse from all other beauty." Edwards, *Religious Affections*, vol. 2 of *The Works of Jonathan Edwards*, ed. John E. Smith (New Haven, CT: Yale University Press, 1959), 298.

independent of us, though we are never independent of God.[11] To put it another way, creation and Creator do not relate to one another as independent realities; creation derives its being and *telos* from the Creator.[12] God displays his beauty, not because it meets his need but because it meets our need. Creation, then, is a superfluous act of generosity on the part of God.

Applying this principle to his acts of creation, we would argue that the most loving thing God can do for creation is to reveal himself, as he alone is beauty and the source of all delight and joy (Exod 3:14–16; Isa 46:9–10).[13] Not only is God's act in creation an act of love, but it is also an act of grace. John Webster captures this belief well when writing that God "could be without the world; no perfection of God would be lost, no triune bliss compromised, were the world not to exist; no enhancement of God is achieved by the world's existence."[14] This belief also informs the inherent essence of beauty in created order "because it derives from God, and therefore exists independent of any creaturely percipient, that is, whether or not is it perceived."[15] Yet, as we saw in chapter 3, God *has* made

---

[11] See Christopher Holmes, *A Theology of the Christian Life: Imitating and Participating in God* (Grand Rapids: Baker Academic, 2021), 137.

[12] See Samuel G. Parkison, *Irresistible Beauty: Beholding Triune Glory in the Face of Jesus Christ* (UK: Christian Focus Publications, 2022), 49–101.

[13] See David Bentley Hart, *The Beauty of the Infinite: The Aesthetics of Christian Truth* (Grand Rapids: Eerdmans, 2003), 177.

[14] John Webster, *God without Measure: Working Papers in Christian Theology*, vol. 1, *God and the Works of God* (London: T&T Clark, 2016), 91.

[15] Jonathan King, *The Beauty of the Lord: Theology as Aesthetics* (Bellingham, WA: Lexham, 2018), 13.

himself known in creation (Rom 1:20). Creation itself testifies to the glory of its Creator (Ps 19:1). Thus, God has made his beauty perceivable!

At its very heart then, the essence of true Christian affection is to perceive and be irresistibly drawn to and overwhelmed by the beauty of the triune God. Consider Augustine, who argued, "To think about God, and about all things in God, as with thinking about beauty. . . . When this theologian speaks of God, he speaks of Beauty, and when he speaks of what is beautiful in this world, he constantly points to the One who is the source and goal of all that is beautiful."[16] Again, "It was you then, O Lord, who made [all things]. You who are beautiful, for they too are beautiful. You who are good, for they too are good. You who are, for they too are. But they are not beautiful and good as you are beautiful and good. Nor do they have their being as you, their Creator, have your being. In comparison with you, they have neither beauty nor goodness nor being at all."[17] This is an indispensable and corrective assertion concerning our study, namely that we begin with a top-down rather than bottom-up approach to our examination of beauty, aesthetics, and spiritual formation. After all, theology is the study of God and then all things in relation to him, and we move along aesthetic experiences like following a sunbeam to the sun. Jonathan Edwards clarifies:

> In the creatures' knowing, esteeming, loving, rejoicing in, and praising God, the glory of God is both exhibited

---

[16] Bruno Forte, *The Portal of Beauty: Towards a Theology of Aesthetics* (Grand Rapids: Eerdmans, 2008), 2.

[17] Augustine, *Confessions*, trans. R. S. Pine-Coffin (New York: Penguin, 1961), 231.

> and acknowledged; his fulness is received and returned. Here is both the *emanation* and *remanation*. The refulgence shines upon and into the creature, and is reflected back to the luminary. The beams of glory come from God, and are something of God and are refunded back again to their original. So that the whole is of God and in God, and to God, and God is the beginning, middle and end in this affair.[18]

A distinctly Christian aesthetic holds that God is the ultimate object of the study in beauty because he is its self-revealing beautiful subject. However, when we speak of God's self-disclosure, we understand from Scripture that God is ultimately incomprehensible and his greatness unsearchable (Job 26:14; 42:1–6; Ps 139:6, 17–18; 145:3, 147:5; Isa 55:8–9; 57:15; Rom 11:33–34; 1 Cor 2:10–11; 1 Tim 6:13–16). Returning to Thomas Aquinas again, "Nothing our understanding can conceive of God succeeds in representing him, so that which is proper to God himself remains hidden to us, and the highest knowledge we can have of him as we live out our journey here on earth lies in recognizing that God is above everything we can think of him."[19] In this sense, we could posit that what God reveals of his beauty is in excess of what hides behind its appearance. And while we cannot behold God exhaustively, Scripture teaches us that God can be known sufficiently, both truly and personally (1 Cor 2:2; Heb 8:11–12; 2 Pet 1:2–3).

---

[18] Jonathan Edwards, *A Dissertation Concerning the End for Which God Created the World* (Carlisle, PA: Banner of Truth Trust, 1995), 120.

[19] Thomas Aquinas, *De Veritate* 2, 1, ad 9m. See Forte, *The Portal of Beauty*, 21.

Therefore, while God is transcendent, wholly and distinctly separate from the created world, he is also immanent, graciously revealing himself in the created world. We know this because in the progress of redemptive history, God has revealed himself in part, piece by piece. God condescends to us in this way because no one could fully see or comprehend God if he were to reveal all that he is. While we cannot see God's beauty fully at present, we can glimpse it as a refraction of his nature. One might liken God's self-disclosure in the way that light passes through a prism. As Peter Sammons describes, "The light is one, but when it passes through a prism it refracts into different rays and colors."[20] Consider Moses, who desired to behold the glory of God but was only permitted to see the aftereffects of God passing by because, as the text says, no one can see God and live (Exod 33:20). As we move along the axis of redemptive history with God revealing himself progressively over time, we reach the New Testament and find an answer to the psalmist's longing "to gaze upon the beauty of the LORD" (Ps 27:4 ESV) in the incarnation of the divine Son, Jesus Christ.

The Beauty of God in the Face of Jesus Christ

This returns us to our top-down approach to beauty because all that has been affirmed from the Old Testament concerning the beauty of God reaches its revelatory crescendo in the incarnation of Jesus Christ, whom the prophet Isaiah spoke of as the beautiful one who was to come to us (Isa 4:2; 28:5; 33:17).

---

[20] See Peter Sammons, *The Forgotten Attributes of God: God's Nature and Why It Matters* (Washington, PA: CLC, 2023), 71.

Before coming to us (for he is before all things), the creative act was by him, through him, and for him; and "by him all things hold together" (Col 1:16–17). Indeed, the world was created for this very end, for God to communicate himself in an image of his own excellency.[21] For this reason, we don't just read the Genesis account as a narrative about the act of creation itself but about our triune God's process of incarnation. With Christ's coming, our eternal God became flesh and made himself "sense perceptible" in creation so that we might be captured by his beauty.[22] In the Old Testament when God came to Mount Sinai, the people of Israel heard God and were afraid but "didn't see a form" (Deut 4:12). Yet, in the New Testament, most clearly on the Mount of Transfiguration, the disciples saw Jesus and were afraid *because* of his form, that is, his irradiant appearance and brilliant luminescence. The optical phenomenon of Jesus's transfiguration was the "visual verification" of his divinity.[23] In other words, the transfiguration marks a point in which God's unveiled glory is expressed most fittingly in and through the form of the Son's humanity. Yet his divine beauty was not only seen on the Mount but also in the valleys of Jesus's comings and goings during his earthly ministry.

In Jesus's teachings, we discover a beautiful resonance to the penetrating truth in his words and in his power over demonic beings, so much so that the religious leaders of his day were astonished at his speaking as one with divine authority

---

[21] See Jonathan Edwards, *The Works of Jonathan Edwards*, vol. 13 (New Haven, CT: Yale University Press, 1992), 279.

[22] Forte, *The Portal of Beauty*, 10.

[23] Craig Evans, *Word Biblical Commentary: Mark 8:27–16:20* (Nashville: Thomas Nelson, 2001), 36.

(Matt 7:29; Mark 1:21–28). When Jesus healed the sick and diseased by his divine power, he pulled back the curtain on the ugliness that mars this broken world to offer us a glimpse of the beautiful world to come.[24] In this sense, miracles enlarge our imaginative capacities and break the immanent frame of nature wide open. But understand, Christ does not simply come to us as a teacher of the truth or just as a useful healer for our own good but to display and radiate his eternal triune beauty. In Christ we see the perfect embodiment of God's beauty in his constancy of character, displaying all his communicable perfections (Col 2:9). Herein lies the beauty of Jesus Christ in perfect holiness. Jonathan Edwards argues, "He is altogether lovely. . . . All the spiritual beauty of his human nature, consisting in his meekness, lowliness, patience, heavenliness, love to God, love to men . . . all is summed up in his holiness. And the beauty of his divine nature, of which the beauty of his human nature is the image and reflection, does primarily consist in his holiness."[25]

---

[24] Jesus healed Peter's sick and fevered mother-in-law (Matt 8:14–15; Mark 1:29–31; Luke 4:38–39), healed all who were sick one evening (Matt 8:16–17; Mark 1:32–34; Luke 4:40–41), cleansed a leper (Matt 8:1–4; Mark 1:40–45; Luke 5:12–14), healed a paralytic who was let down through the roof of a house where Jesus was speaking (Matt 9:1–8; Mark 2:1–12; Luke 5:17–26), and even healed a centurion's servant (Matt 8:5–13; Luke 7:6–10). He healed a man's withered hand—on the Sabbath day no less (Matt 12:9–14; Mark 3:1–6; Luke 6:6–11), raised a widow's son from the dead (Luke 7:11–17), healed a woman who suffered from constant bleeding (Matt 9:20–22; Mark 5:25–34; Luke 8:42–48), healed two blind men (Matt 9:27–31), and these are just a few of his healing miracles.

[25] Edwards, *Religious Affections*, 258.

This is Jesus's transcendent splendor, representing the irruption of the ultimate into the penultimate. It is through the Son incarnate that we also see God's beauty fittingly manifested in a demonstration of self-giving love in truth, goodness, and beauty. In other words, Christ's life is the outward expression of his inward perfection, in both being and doing. To put it another way, Christ exemplifies the highest expression of all moral and spiritual categories. Steve DeWitt notes that when we think of compassion, loving-sacrifice, kindness, wisdom, and integrity—Jesus not only perfectly expresses them; he is the ultimate standard for "every noble characteristic we admire."[26] In Jesus Christ's humanity, the beauty of God is made truly known, personally. As the writer of Hebrews shows us, "Long ago God spoke to our ancestors by the prophets at different times and in different ways. In these last days, he has spoken to us by his Son" (Heb 1:1–2a).

In the Colossian Christological poem, the apostle Paul declares that Jesus Christ "is the image of the invisible God," in whom the "entire fullness of God's nature dwells bodily" (Col 1:15; 2:9). The writer of Hebrews concurs that "the Son is the radiance of God's glory and the exact expression of his nature" (Heb 1:3). Jesus himself makes this explicitly clear in the gospel of John: "If you know me, you will also know my Father. From now on you do know him and have *seen* him" (John 14:7, emphasis added). The Johannine assertion that knowing Christ is equated with seeing God is central to a distinctly Christian aesthetic. After all, when Scripture speaks

---

[26] Steve DeWitt, *Eyes Wide Open: Enjoying God in Everything* (Grand Rapids: Credo, 2011), 104–5.

of God's face, glory, and majesty, it uses sensory or aesthetic language. As Robert Louis Wilken explains, "Beauty is the corollary of seeing. In the Scriptures many of the key terms used of God's self-disclosure, words such as glory, splendor, light, image, and face, have to do with the delight of the eye. When we speak of the pleasure the eye takes in what it sees the term that comes to mind is *beauty*."[27]

Thus, Jesus Christ is the pinnacle of God's beautiful self-expression in creation, the "fleshing out" of Scripture's portrait of God. Therefore, a distinctly Christian aesthetic would posit that ultimate beauty is not originated in the eye of the beholder but in beholding God's beloved son, Jesus Christ. This is precisely what Aquinas taught: "Beauty is concerned with what is proper to the Son."[28] Beauty is beheld when the self-giving of God made himself manifest in the event of the incarnation of the eternal Son, who is beauty in person.[29] All beauties, as well as our aesthetic longings, find their final and perfect embodiment in Jesus Christ. For this reason alone, Christians dare to sing about the beauty of the cross, by which the most hideous sight is received as breathtakingly beautiful.

---

[27] Robert Louis Wilken, *The Spirit of Early Christian Thought: Seeking the Face of God* (New Haven, CT: Yale University Press, 2003), 20.

[28] Thomas Aquinas, *The "Summa Theologica" of St. Thomas of Aquinas*, trans. the Fathers of the English Dominican Province (London: R. & T. Washbourne, 1912), pt. I, q. 39, a. 8c (p. 144).

[29] In philosophical terms, "Beauty itself is amorphous but is known as beauty only when it reveals itself in a formed object." See Jeffrey Ames Kay, *Theological Aesthetics: The Role of Aesthetics in the Theological Method of Hans Urs von Balthasar* (Frankfurt: Herbert Lang and Peter Lang, 1975), 4.

Conclusion

Several questions remain as we conclude the theological reflections explored in this chapter, one regarding nonbelievers and another for believers. First, why is it that many people are blind to God's beauty? Why do nonbelievers find God's self-exalting demands for worship in response to his proclaimed beauty so repulsive and disagreeable? The apostle Paul explains this for us when he argued that "the god of this age has blinded the minds of the unbelievers to keep them from seeing the light of the gospel of the glory of Christ, who is the image of God" (2 Cor 4:4). The simple answer is that many have not been given spiritual eyes to see. This confirms Isaiah's prophecy of Christ's reception as one who "didn't have an impressive form or majesty that we should look at him, no appearance that we should desire him" (Isa 53:2). It is a stumbling block for some to consider divine beauty entering the world as an infant to a poor girl and a common carpenter. Even more, when we typically speak of someone's beauty, we often begin with observations about that person's physical attractiveness. Apart from the transfiguration, however, we are given no information regarding Jesus's appearance in Scripture. Because beauty is integral to God's essential nature, God is not required to conform his self-revelation to our worldly norms and notions of beauty.[30] After all, while God's unveiled glory is expressed most fittingly in and through Jesus Christ, Jesus was not paraded before us with superficial splendor.

Second, for Christians, there are times in our lives when we inhabit what the Celtic Christians called "thin places," where our

---

[30] King, *The Beauty of the Lord,* 209.

sense of the barrier between heaven and earth is porous because the beauty of the Lord is palpable.[31] But too often, our sense of wonderment loses its emotive vitality, and the beauty of God becomes trite in our souls. How often have we entered the cathedral of the Word and read the poetic description of God being "clothed with majesty and splendor" (Ps 104:1) and found ourselves curiously unmoved? Perhaps more than we'd care to admit. This dreadful observation of our progression from awe to indifference is analogous to many Christians' domesticated experience with the living God of the universe. What can we do to strip the veil of familiarity that often covers the eyes of our faith? How can we awaken from our spiritual lethargy and rekindle our wonder for God? How can we once more proclaim with the psalmist that "I desire nothing on earth but you" (Ps 73:25)? What impedes us from perpetually, and undistractedly, gazing upon the Lord's beauty as we joyfully contemplate his loving and gracious character? Well, we are not without hope. Gregory of Nyssa reminds us:

> Hope always draws the soul from the beauty which is seen to what is beyond, always kindles the desire for the hidden through what is constantly perceived. Therefore, the ardent lover of beauty, although receiving what is always visible as an image of what he desires, yet longs to be filled with the very stamp of the archetype. And the bold request which goes up the mountains of desire asks this: to empty the Beauty not in mirrors and reflections, but face to face.[32]

---

[31] Timothy George, "Thin Places," *First Things* (November 2, 2015), https://www.firstthings.com/web-exclusives/2015/11/thin-places.

[32] St. Gregory of Nyssa, *The Life of Moses*, trans. Abraham Malherbe and Everett Ferguson (Mahwah, NJ: Paulist, 1978) 2.32, 114.

The fountainhead of all delights in the Christian life is to "taste and see that the Lord is good" (Ps 34:8), and this spiritual nourishment is found in the face of Jesus Christ, who gives himself without reserve. Indeed, as Clement of Alexandria said, "Our savior is beautiful to be loved by those who desire true beauty."[33] In beholding Christ, or being held by Christ, we perceive God, beauty, and all things beautiful. As Sang Hyun Lee writes, "To know and love God, therefore, is to know and love the beauty of God, and to know the ultimate nature of the world is to know and love the world as an image of God's beauty."[34]

---

[33] Clement of Alexandria, quoted in Patrick Sherry, *Spirit and Beauty: An Introduction to Theological Aesthetics* (London: SCM, 2002), 6.

[34] Sang Hyun Lee, "Edwards and Beauty" in *Understanding Jonathan Edwards: An Introduction to America's Theologian*, ed. Gerald McDermott (New York: Oxford University Press, 2009), 113.

5

Prone to Wander, Pardoned to Wonder

From Bondage to Beholding His Beauty

As it is difficult to convey an idea of color to the blind, or of music to the deaf, so it is difficult to describe to a natural man the peculiar perceptions of one whose eyes have been opened by the Spirit. And the difficulty is not diminished but increased by the fact, that he has a kind of knowledge which is common to him with the true believer, and which is too apt to be mistaken for that which the Gospel requires. Perhaps the nearest approach that we can make to an explanation may be by asking you to conceive of a man who sees, but has no sense of beauty, or of a man who hears, but has no sense of harmony; just such is the case of a natural man, who sees the truth without perceiving its spiritual excellence, and on whose ear the sound of the Gospel falls without awakening music in his soul.

—*James Buchanan*, The Office and Work of the Holy Spirit

Through a Glass, Darkly

It was in a stuffy and dimly lit lecture hall of an art history course that I, along with approximately sixty other university students, was introduced to the work of Robert Mapplethorpe. The lecture included a presentation of the provocative pictures of the photographer's late 1980s exhibition titled *The Perfect Moment*. The photographs were a mixture of seductive nude portraits, flower arrangements, and obscene depictions of homosexual sadomasochism. In the art world, the initial showing of the retrospective of the artist's career was met with both enthusiastic critical acclaim and appalling moral outrage. Long before it reached the university lecture hall, Mapplethorpe's work infamously ignited a censorship battle that eventually made its way to Congress.

After that class, I remember discussing the content of *The Perfect Moment* exhibition with a fellow Christian art student as we walked across the university courtyard. He woefully uttered something along the lines of, "I'll never look at flowers the same way again." After all, within the context of the exhibition, flowers that—for us—had once only signified the sweetness of God's benevolence were depicted alongside explicit portraits and were now framed as sensual forms that evoked crude sexual desire. As Christians, we lamented the fact that a collection including pornographic images had led many secular art critics to regard Mapplethorpe as a giant among the avant-garde of artists in the twentieth century. While Mapplethorpe undoubtedly demonstrated acute aesthetic sensibilities in his work, he unfortunately also pushed the moral boundaries of the art world and, in doing so, exposed our depraved disposition to corrupt even the most innocent and natural of objects.[1] However, what Mapplethorpe represented in his cultural milieu was not a problem that originated in the modern art studio or gallery but in the garden of Eden. It was humanity's fall that introduced all of humanity to sin, thus deforming our perception of beauty and aesthetics altogether. Since the fall, we have never experienced beauty the same way. As the psalmist wrote, "The light has gone from my eyes" (Ps 38:10 NIV). The apostle Paul reminds us that, post-fall, we humans only "see through a glass, darkly" (1 Cor 13:12 KJV). Because we have a warped spiritual condition, we also have a distorted sense of perception. We often feel this tension in our daily life, don't we? Our world is not always beautiful in the purest sense. Great terror and ugliness mar the scene, a reality that can impart disillusionment and nihilism. What, then, of this darkened distortion?

The Fall of Man, Sin, and Aesthetic Depravity

Scripture teaches us that the initial disobedience of Adam and Eve in Genesis 3 resulted in the corruption of all creation and in all people being born into sin.[2] Post-fall, the whole sphere of human activities has since been tainted by the twisting of our depravity. Sinfulness seeps into every crevice of human

---

[1] Arguably, the most comprehensive indictment of our modern cultural ethos is found in Carl Trueman's *The Rise and Triumph of the Modern Self: Cultural Amnesia, Expressive Individualism, and the Road to Sexual Revolution* (Wheaton, IL: Crossway, 2020).

[2] In this section we cannot fully examine the doctrine of sin (*hamartiology*) and will focus our attention on its effects on beauty and our perception in aesthetics.

existence; it darkens the intellect and disorders the affections. Just as with any other aspect of human life, beauty and aesthetics can and often have taken a dark turn in the hearts of sinful humans. The reason is that the fall brings estrangement from God, and this alienation becomes the source of all sin (Ps 51:3–4). If God is the origin and author of all beauty, then sin's destruction of that order ruptures and obscures all things, including aesthetic experiences. Thus, there is now a tension between the clarity of God's disclosure in aesthetic experiences and the distortion of it by fallen humanity.[3] As Michael Bird argues, we must concede that sinful persons suppress the knowledge of God in creation, which is now "hardly neutral or self-evident."[4] To quote Christopher Holmes, "Our senses and our intellect err when we forget our cause and end. They can no longer fulfill their God-given function by pointing us to their Creator. We cannot see things as they are."[5] By implication, Barth adds, "There is no territory which has been spared and where he does not sin, where he is not perverted, where he still maintains the divine order and is therefore guiltless."[6] By our sinful nature, then, when it comes to all beauty and aesthetic experiences, we not only fail to see God's beauty; we often "take what God creates and calls 'good'—and we twist and pervert it until it becomes only a hollow shell that retains just enough

---

[3] See Russell D. Moore, "Natural Revelation," in *A Theology for the Church*, ed. Daniel L. Akin (Nashville: B&H, 2007), 71.

[4] Michael Bird, *Evangelical Theology* (Grand Rapids: Zondervan, 2013), 72.

[5] Christopher R. J. Holmes, *A Theology of the Christian Life* (Grand Rapids: Baker Academic, 2021), 20.

[6] Karl Barth, *Church Dogmatics*, vol. 4, part 1 (London: T&T Clark, 2004), 496.

resemblance of the original good to serve as a mocking taunt."[7] Therefore, the arts are of great interest to the spiritual forces of evil.

In our fallen world, God's beauty is often parodied, warped, and distorted. It is no wonder that we divert the Edenic construction materials initially given for the city of God for use in the side project of our own desires and glory, twisting those materials to serve an unworthy end.[8] The Tower of Babel illustrates the perversion of architecture as a means to glorify man (Gen 11:1–9). The idolatry of Aaron's calf illustrates the ease with which humanity can pervert the artist's gift and elevate a sculpture to godlike status, exchanging the glory of God for man-made images (Exodus 32; Rom 1:21–23). Even fiction becomes heretical pagan myth, of which Paul warned Timothy (1 Tim 1:3–4). Indeed, our fallen nature means that aesthetic experience, the perception of beauty, and the arts can have an immoral effect on their audience. If we consider our sinful nature and its twisting of beautiful and aesthetic experiences, we must take into account how these things form us as spiritual beings. For this reason, the doctrine of sin alone should give any Christian pause in heartily agreeing with the postmodern relativism associated with one of David Hume's most enduring philosophical contributions, the idea that beauty is in the eye of the beholder, for it cannot be reduced to that alone.[9]

---

[7] Thomas H. McCall, *Against God and Nature: The Doctrine of Sin* (Wheaton, IL: Crossway, 2019), 231.

[8] See Cornelius Plantinga, *Not the Way It's Supposed to Be: A Breviary of Sin* (Grand Rapids: Eerdmans, 1996), 40.

[9] See David Hume's *Essays, Moral and Political* (Indianapolis: Liberty Fund, 1985). In essay XXIII ("Of the Standard of Taste"), Hume argues that a thousand different sentiments can be excited by

The Beauty of Christ and the Aesthetics of the Cross

The writers of Scripture often favored the metaphor of "seeing" in relation to "beholding" God, and pure beauty is the result of seeing him as he is (Matt 5:8). Still, in our natural depraved state, we are all blinded to God's glory (2 Cor 4:4). John tells us that no one who abides in him sins and that the one who does sin "has not *seen* him or known him" (1 John 3:6, emphasis added). He goes on to say that "the one who does evil has not *seen* God" (3 John 11, emphasis added). This is where our study of beauty and aesthetics turns toward the eternal devastation that awaits those who reject God's goodness in unbelief. The horror of being God-forsaken comes with a burning and gnawing remorse in the final recognition of God's undeniable worth, goodness, and beauty. Devoid of any joy and delight, the damned will no longer be able to offer praise but will only curse God for all of eternity. For those in hell, the only experience of God's presence will be found in punishment. Amos 9:14 gives us a vivid description of God's presence in judgment. In judgment,

---

the same object, and they are all right. "No sentiment represents what is really in the object. It only marks a certain conformity or relation between the object and the organs or faculties of the mind; and if that conformity did not really exist, the sentiment could never possibly have being. Beauty is no quality in things themselves: it exists merely in the mind which contemplates them; and each mind perceives a different beauty. One person may even perceive deformity, where another is sensible of beauty; and every individual ought to acquiesce in his own sentiment, without pretending to regulate those of others. To seek the real beauty, or real deformity, is as fruitless an enquiry, as to pretend to ascertain the real sweet or real bitter."

the eyes of the condemned will be finally opened but opened only in the torment of regret. Imagine an eternity without the experience of God's goodness (Prov 15:29; Isa 59:2). Imagine an eternity devoid of any beauty or aesthetic pleasure. The question before us, then, is how can we move beyond the secondary and obscured beauties of this world toward the One who is beautiful in himself, namely, God? How can our eyes be opened to see?

Jesus's words in John 9:39 are of particular interest here: "I came into this world . . . [so] that those who do not see will *see*" (emphasis added). Paul strikes a similar note in 2 Corinthians 4, stating that the natural man is blind to the light of the gospel of the glory of Christ, who is the image of God. However, the same God who said, "Let light shine out of darkness" has "shone in our hearts to give the light of the knowledge of God's glory in the face of Jesus Christ" (2 Cor 4:4–6). For it is through the person and work of Christ, as Augustine argues, that "eternal beauty becomes flesh and makes itself perceptible to the sense of our outward selves, so that our inner selves might be touched and captured by the grace which frees and saves us."[10] Aquinas adds that, in the Son, "the whole bursts forth, allowing God's beauty to be most present and perceptible for humanity—the irruption of the ultimate into the penultimate."[11] Therefore, pure beauty

---

[10] Bruno Forte, *The Portal of Beauty: Towards a Theology of Aesthetics* (Grand Rapids: Eerdmans, 2008), 10.

[11] Thomas Aquinas, *Summa Theologica* I, q. 39, a. 8c. There are three things that must be present for beauty to exist according to Aquinas, namely, perfection, harmony, and luminosity. These theories of Aquinas are explored in *Summa Theologica* (Ia, q. 73, a. 1C). For a thorough explanation of them, see Umberto Eco, *The Aesthetics of Thomas Aquinas* (Cambridge, MA: Harvard University Press, 1988). For Aquinas, perfection in beauty is the form of the whole, which issues from the perfection

is not situated in the eye of the beholder but in beholding God's beloved Son, Jesus Christ.

Returning to our top-down approach, since God brought creation into being for his glory, it is fitting and gracious that he would provide a way to reach this end (Heb 2:10). That "way" is mediated through Christ alone, for in Christ, we are presented with God's most beautiful revelation. The Christian tradition maintains that we contemplate this beauty through the crucified, risen, and glorified Christ.[12] John Calvin articulates this reality wonderfully:

> For in the cross of Christ, as in a magnificent theatre, the inestimable goodness of God is displayed before the whole world. In all the creatures, indeed, both high and low, the glory of God shines, but nowhere has it shone more brightly than in the cross, in which there has been an astonishing change of things, the condemnation of all men has been manifested, sin has been blotted out, a salvation has been restored to men; and, in short, the whole world has been renewed, and everything restored to good order.[13]

---

of the parts. The Son is the perfect representation of the whole in part. As for harmony, Aquinas argued that beauty is found in the fragment, which represents itself in relationship with the parts present in the whole. In this way, beauty dwells in the Son because it is common to the nature of the Trinity. Last, he explored luminosity as the instance when beauty gloriously breaks from the whole, upon us in part. The Son is clothed in the beauty of the whole which shines forth in Jesus's splendor.

[12] See John Navone, *Toward a Theology of Beauty* (Collegeville, PA: Liturgical, 1996), v.

[13] John Calvin, *Commentary on the Gospel According to John*, vol. 2 (Eugene, OR: Wipf and Stock, 2016), 73.

Still, there is a sense in which "the horror of the cross screams against every sensibility" of our aesthetic.[14] On the one hand, the cross of Christ offers a beauty that is perfectly fitting against the collective crime committed against him, as he bore the ugliness of all our sin and endured the indignities of this fallen world. And on the other hand, it is the most potent and beautiful expression of God's self-giving.[15] Simply put, the cross of Christ is both the most grotesque monstrosity the world has ever known and, at the same time, God's greatest masterpiece ever to be displayed. Christ's suffering on the cross becomes beautiful to those who have eyes to see because it was vicarious (on behalf of others) and salvific (for a redemptive purpose).[16] Remember, all of God's acts are perfectly fitting in accordance with his purposes, and everything he does is beautifully God-glorifying. And as we have seen, his glory is for our good. This is why Augustine argues, "He hung . . . on the cross deformed, and His deformity is our beauty."[17] The good news of the gospel is that Jesus came to liberate us *from* our bondage to decay and liberate us *to* behold his divine beauty (Rom 8:21).

While the beauty of the cross is always before us, it is not always perceived by everyone. For those familiar with the trends of the modern art world, Robert Mapplethorpe was not unique in pushing moral and religious boundaries. In the same era,

---

[14] Adapted from Philip Ryken, *Beauty Is Your Destiny: How the Promise of Splendor Changes Everything* (Wheaton, IL: Crossway, 2023) 114.

[15] See Richard Viladesau, *Theological Aesthetics* (New York: Oxford University Press, 1999), 189–97.

[16] See Francis M. DuBose, *God Who Sends: A Fresh Quest for Biblical Mission* (Nashville: Baptist Sunday School Board, 1983), 95.

[17] Augustine, Sermon xxvii, 6, PL 38:181.

New York artist Andres Serrano photographed a plastic crucifix plunged into a glass of his own urine and titled it "Piss Christ." For Serrano, the complex imagery of the "Piss Christ" represented his unresolved feelings about his Catholic upbringing, as well as the desecrating commodification of the cross. However, for many of the religious, "Piss Christ" was seen not only as a rebellion against classical conceptions of art but also as a sacrilegious affront to the beauty of the cross of our Lord as depicted in symbol.[18] Recently, Pope Francis held a gathering of artists from thirty countries to address the long-standing relationship between the church and the arts. During the gathering, the pope observed that art plumbs "the depths of the human condition, its dark abysses. We are not all light, and you remind us of this."[19] Ironically, Serrano was in attendance.

The Beauty That Is to Come

This reminds us of the deeper truth that all our personal problems and all the evils of history are related to our depraved inability to see and know without divine intervention how beautiful God is. Again, we need "eyes to see" (see Matt 13:16). The good news is that within the economy of the Trinity, "the glory of the

---

[18] Lucy Lippard, "From the Archives: Andres Serrano, The Spirit and the Letter," *Art in America*, January 5, 2023, https://www.artnews.com/art-in-america/features/andres-serrano-provocative-work-lucy-lippard-1234652353/.

[19] Hannah Brockhaus, "Pope Francis Addresses Artists, Including Creator of Blasphemous Crucifix Photo," Catholic News Agency, June 23, 2023, https://www.catholicnewsagency.com/news/254648/pope-francis-addresses-artists-including-creator-of-blasphemous-crucifix-photo.

Father is manifested through his Word and Image, the Son, and the Holy Spirit leads us to see that manifested glory."[20] In other words, the glory of God is diffused through the Holy Spirit as the beautifier within the Trinity, and he gives us the eyes to see. The Christian tradition has long held that for one to break free from the blindness caused by sin, the beauty of God in Christ must be revealed by the Holy Spirit (1 Cor 2:9–11). While the cross of Christ exposes us to our own moral ugliness, it is by the Spirit that we become open to his beautifying grace.[21] Thus the human beholder is brought to perception only by God's grace, given the "eyes of faith" to perceive what he or she could not see before, the objective beauty of the person of Jesus Christ. We might call this a divinely granted "sense" for beauty.[22] In other words, by God's Spirit alone do we perceive Jesus rightly, to grow in delight of God's beauty, and to understand the beauty of our world.[23]

This is perfectly fitting, just as in creation when we consider that the Holy Spirit fashioned the world into a beautiful place out of the chaos. The Holy Spirit continues to bring the world and everything in it—including humanity—out of chaos to beauty and perfection. Jesuit theologian John Navone captures this reality delightfully: "In Jesus Christ, the perfect image of God, Beauty itself appears and grasps us in the very act of overwhelming us by his ineffable love. Jesus Christ is the concrete form through which the splendor of God irradiates and transfigures

---

[20] Patrick Sherry, *Spirit and Beauty: An Introduction to Theological Aesthetics* (London, SCM, 2002), 72.

[21] See Jonathan Edwards, *The Works of Jonathan Edwards*, vol. 2 (New Haven, CT: Yale University Press, 1992), 50.

[22] Jonathan Edwards, *Treatise on Grace*, ed. Paul Helm (Cambridge, UK: James Clarke, 1988), 49.

[23] See Sherry, *Spirit and Beauty*, 12.

humankind so that, through the gift of his Spirit, we become . . . beautiful in Beauty itself."[24] The Holy Spirit then enables all with faith to subjectively experience and grow in delight of the objective beauty of God. As the apostle Paul proclaims, the Spirit enables one to see the beauty of God in "the light of the gospel of the glory of Christ, who is the image of God" (2 Cor 4:4).

The New Heavens and New Earth

This beautifying work of the Spirit presents an eschatological significance as well, "in that it is the anticipation of the restored and transfigured world in which will be the fullness of God's kingdom."[25] As we are poised between creation and new creation, a part of the eschatological gestation of redemptive history, it is important to be reminded that the biblical witness testifies of Christ's coming to bring into existence a new creation. In the Gospel accounts, the resurrection marks the moment when beauty's power is not only revealed in its fullest manifestation but is the firstfruits of the beautiful world to come. As Christ ascends to the Father, we begin to understand his words in John 12:32: "When I am lifted up from the earth, [I] will draw all people to myself" (NIV). This eschatological vision of Christ points forward to the time when divine beauty is made fully manifest to man, not just temporarily but permanently for all eternity. The hope of beholding the Lord's beauty in the second coming of Christ involves all of God's people being changed in the blissful moment of seeing Christ "face to face" (1 John 3:2 NIV; see also 1 Cor 13:12; 15:51–52; 2 Cor 3:18; Rev 22:4). At

---

[24] Navone, *Toward a Theology of Beauty*, 21–22.

[25] Sherry, *Spirit and Beauty*, 161.

the sight of Christ's divine beauty, we will become like what we behold. Theologians often refer to this eschatological apprehension of Christ as the "beatific vision."[26]

This powerful transformation through simply "seeing" Christ in all of his splendor elicits liberation from the decay of sin, the cosmos being made new, and the transfiguration of his children through their own easter morning (Isa 61:3; Rom 8:18–19; Phil 3:20–21; Rev 21:5). Even more, the glorification of God's people and the renewal of creation are directly related (Gen 3:14–19; Rom 8:18–25). The New Testament descriptions suggest that believers' glorified bodies will possess a beauty, attractiveness, and even radiance as a reflection of the beauty of Christ. Wayne Grudem captures this eschatological longing well: "When we realize that God is the perfection of all we long for or desire, that he is the summation of everything beautiful or desirable, then we realize that the greatest joy of the life to come will be that we 'shall see his face'."[27] In the end, seeing the beauty of Christ will bring God's children into full aesthetic delight and eternal joy, as part of the glittering finale of new creation (Ps 16:11). On that day, we will fully appreciate the beauty of God as we are fully glorified in him. Imagine, the One who sits on the throne of the universe has the appearance of jasper, and a rainbow resembling an emerald encircled the throne (Rev 4:3). Even the Holy City, the final estate prepared for God's people, will be gloriously adorned as a beautiful bride for her husband with precious stones (Rev 21:2).

---

[26] "Beatific" comes from two Latin words meaning "blessed" (*beatus*) and "to make" (*facere*).

[27] Wayne A. Grudem, *Systematic Theology: An Introduction to Biblical Doctrine* (Grand Rapids: Zondervan, 2009), 190.

Conclusion: Enraptured in Eternity

With this in mind, we should hardly be surprised that beauty plays such an important role in the Bible's eschatological trajectory. The biblical writers declared that God is a crown of beauty for his faithful remnant, which is more significant than simple attractiveness and is synonymous with all that encompasses God's glory. Scripture beckons God's people to long with an expectation of basking in his beauty, a full vision of God who, up to this point, has only been known in part (Isa 28:5; 1 Cor 2:9). It is hard to imagine beholding, or "being held," by God's unimaginable splendor. In a sense, this is what Balthasar longed for, the day in which we would quiver before our beautiful God, not only finding his beauty moving but also "being moved and possessed by it."[28] For now, we can only dream of dwelling in a new creation, the gardens of God's delight. As Jonathan King says, "What life will be like in the age to come for the children of God is one of those wonderful imponderables. In the same way, we can be certain that on this side of the veil what we know and experience of beauty in all its expressions will be transcended beyond what we can even possibly conceive of and imagine."[29]

The very thought of such a thing evokes the purest response of worship. The English poet John Donne helps us sense the eternal pleasures of beholding the infinite God, whose beauty is inexhaustible.[30] Donne says, "No man ever saw God and lived.

---

[28] Hans Urs von Balthasar, *The Glory of the Lord: A Theological Aesthetics* (San Francisco: Ignatius, 2009), 247.

[29] Jonathan King, *The Beauty of the Lord: Theology as Aesthetics* (Bellingham, WA: Lexham, 2018), 322.

[30] Benjamin P. Myers, *A Poetics of Orthodoxy: Christian Truth as Aesthetic Foundation* (Eugene, OR: Wipf and Stock, 2020), 70.

And yet, I shall not live till I see God. And when I have seen him, I shall never die."[31]

This is what Bavinck speaks of as the "brilliant unfading splendor," that we will not transcend our humanity but will transcend the bondage of death and "[blossom] in a springtime of eternal youth."[32] Amazing, isn't it? This is God's intent for humanity. His work in this present age is that of making his children beautiful, conforming them to the image of his Son (Rom 8:19–23; 1 Cor 15:48–49; 2 Cor 3:18; Eph 4:22–24; 5:27; 1 John 3:1–2). God's goal is that his children would be adorned and formed as a beautiful bride in preparation for her eternal union with Christ, beautified by being progressively formed in his image (1 Cor 11:1; 2 Cor 3:18; Eph 4:22–24; 5:1–2; 1 Pet 2:21; 1 John 2:6). This is the beauty of the gospel: our Christian pilgrimage begins with God, seeing him as the source and substance of all beauty, and our pilgrimage ends with God, seeing him in all of his beauty face to face.[33] On that day we will be enraptured by God. We will be drenched in beauty. And it will be an experience that never ends.

---

[31] John Donne, "Sermon Preached to the Lords upon Easter-day, at the Communion, 1619" in *The Works of John Donne*, ed. Henry Alford (np), sermon XCV, 238.

[32] Herman Bavinck, *Reformed Dogmatics*, ed. John Bolt, vol. 4, *Holy Spirit, Church, and New Creation* (Grand Rapids: Baker Academic, 2008), 720.

[33] See Christopher R. J. Holmes, *A Theology of the Christian Life: Imitating and Participating in God* (Grand Rapids: Baker Academics, 2021), 3.

6

Christians, the True Aesthetes

Imaging God in Our Being and Making

What moves me is the idea that God has the heart of an artist, . . . The thought of seeing every person, ourselves included, as a unique work of art in progress, an ever-changing and matchless expression of God, changes everything.

—*Martin Schleske*, The Sound of Life's Unspeakable Beauty

Chance or Intent?

Several years ago on a cool winter night, Laura and I were invited by some friends to attend the annual holiday performance of Handel's *Messiah* at Duke University Chapel. As we entered the chapel, our conversation and laughter quieted down, and our posture turned to hallowed reverence. Once seated, we found ourselves enclosed and enchanted by dwarfing chapel walls that drew our eyes upward. Illuminated stained-glass panels, soaring arches, embroidered cloths, and wood embellishments added to the overwhelming sense of "otherworldliness." It was our first visit to Duke Chapel, and it was an enrapturing evening as the chapel choir recreated the renowned composer's masterwork accompanied by an orchestra with Baroque period instruments and intermittent readings of Holy Scripture. The oratorio was stunning in its own right, but the experience was undoubtedly enhanced by the sounds of the vocalists and instrumentalists echoing through the towers of the English Gothic sanctuary.

This is precisely why the architects of Duke University's Chapel meticulously fashioned this religious space as they did, to arouse this sense of sacred transcendence in anyone who entered. It is this mutual exchange between the artisans (architects, craftsman, musicians) and the audience that speaks to the mysterious wonder of the human experience. With the sacred space and melodic sounds of a truly beautiful moment, the barrier between heaven and earth becomes porous. These experiences are an apt reminder that human beings are aesthetic creatures possessed with the distinct capacity for aesthetic sensibility and endowed with the ability to enjoy and create beautiful things. Embedded in this reality is the question of this endowment: Is it an implication of chance or of created intent? This is a question for which the Christian tradition offers an answer.

What, Then, of Aesthetic Endowment?

Thinkers have pondered beauty and aesthetic experiences for millennia, and modern secular schools of thought have produced several theories in an attempt to clarify our unique and distinct capacity for such things. Some scholars have attempted to hang their thoughts on evolutionary instinct. For these thinkers, beauty primarily serves to enhance humanity's chance of survival or to strengthen its social bonds. On the one hand, these people might explain the attractiveness of certain landscapes by their abundance of natural resources for food, water, and shelter. However, this does not account for the gratuitous beauty that adorns much of creation. One may be drawn toward the vibrant pink and green ornamentation of a central American pitaya cactus, but its beauty is not necessary for the nutritional value found in the fruit it produces. On the other hand, these scholars might point to the mutual awe shared by a group of friends in delighting in a sunset or in the participation of rituals that utilize singing, instrumentation, or dance. But to argue that the enjoyment of aesthetic experiences is a by-product of social conditioning does not account for the fact that infants are attracted to certain objects because of the complexity and color and light. Young children across the globe voluntarily begin drawing and singing on their own.

Throughout human history, beauty has been experienced across cultures by people with different aesthetic sensibilities and capacities. The human capacity to create beautiful things is displayed not only in the oil paintings in the Louvre but also in the crayon drawings in the elementary classrooms of rural Louisiana. Granted, the creation of social bonds and survival-enhancing benefits of beauty are true in as much as they are observations about the power of aesthetic experiences and our desire to cultivate beauty around us. In the end, however, the argument that beauty and aesthetic experience come by chance, a mere by-product of evolution or social conditioning, is unsatisfactory, a stretch to say the least.[1] It is even demeaning, as if humans were a kind of beast with no innate constitution for aesthetic sensibility. Even if we recognize that perceptions of what constitutes the beautiful are often culturally conditioned, what we find beautiful is often filtered by how we have learned to perceive it. Our aesthetic becomes a matter of listening to the right voices.[2] As Christians, we would contend that the cultivation and benefits of beauty are a secondary implication of our created intent and a subjective experience that is derivative of an objective reality.

Imagining God in Creation

On November 15, 2007, an oil painting titled *Salvator Mundi* (Latin for "Savior of the World") sold for just over $450 million at Christie's auction house in Britain, setting a new record for the most expensive work of art ever sold in a public auction. The painting has a certain serenity to it, as Jesus is depicted in Renaissance clothes, offering the calming sign of blessing with his right hand, effortlessly holding the entire cosmos in his left. The painting, however, has not been without controversy as its

---

[1] See Anjan Chatterjee's *The Aesthetic Brain: How We Evolved to Desire Beauty and Enjoy Art* (Oxford, UK: Oxford University Press, 2015).

[2] In *Mountain Gloom and Mountain Glory*, Marjorie Hope Nicolson offers a fascinating perspective on how others' voices shape our perceptions of beauty as she considers the intellectual renaissance of the Romantic poets, who sang in praise of mountain splendor and of glorious heights that stirred souls toward divine ecstasy. See *Mountain Gloom and Mountain Glory: The Development of Aesthetics of the Infinite* (Seattle: University of Washington Press, 1997).

attribution to the Italian master Leonardo da Vinci has been both affirmed and disputed by art scholars and Renaissance specialists. There have been numerous paintings that bear the likeness of the *Salvator Mundi,* but in this case, the auctioned painting's value was ascribed exclusively to the identity of the artist who supposedly painted it, da Vinci. In art theory, a particular piece reflects the external *sitz im leben* ("setting of life") of the artist. Undoubtedly, cultural appropriations and theological presuppositions are embedded in the details of the *Salvator Mundi*. Art also serves to express the internal state and values of its creator. In many ways, this analogy helps us understand our own selves as beings created in God's image. If our study of beauty and aesthetics begins with God and relates all things back to him, then our value and purpose as human beings are embedded in our doctrine.

The Christian tradition would hold that we, as humans, hold a particular value *because* of the One who created us. While all things are created by God, humans are distinct within creation as the only beings created in the "image of God." Even the words of the Genesis creation account signal this distinction regarding man in the phrase "let us make," an intentional shift in language as compared to the words "let there be" used for the rest of creation.[3] While God ascribes "goodness" to his creation, the words "very good" are reserved for humans alone. These verbal cues indicate that we as humans are the highest creatures on earth, the culmination of God's creation.[4] While

[3] See Gen 1:26–27 as compared to Gen 1:1–25.

[4] Even cosmologists, when considering the precision of the universe, acknowledge what has been called the "anthropic principle," namely, that our planet is fine-tuned for our existence. See Thomas Dubay, *Evidential Power of Beauty: Science and Beauty Meet* (San Francisco: Ignatius, 1999), 212.

theologians have long debated what exactly being created in the "image of God" consists of, one way to broadly define this "image" is as a distinct resemblance, representation, and reflection.[5] Thus, as beings created in the image of God, humans are specifically endowed with physical, moral, and mental qualities as well as aesthetic sensibilities. And a distinct capacity for beauty—among other things—is bestowed on humans alone. R. Albert Mohler concurs, "This desire for and recognition of beauty is something unique to human beings. Dogs do not contemplate a sunset. Animals do not ponder the beauty of a landscape. It is true the heavens are declaring the glory of God, but most of the creatures on the planet are oblivious to this fact."[6] The Christian tradition has demonstrated its credibility in its consistency of this observation. In fact, Mohler echoes the sentiment of Augustine, who posited that "beauty should be self-evident to all who are of sound mind."[7]

Then why does beauty not speak to everyone in the same way? Animals both small and large see it, but they cannot form a question about it. In them, reason does not sit in judgment upon the deliverances of the senses. But human beings can ask a question so that "the invisible things of God are understood

[5] See John S. Hammett and Katie J. McCoy's *Humanity* (Nashville: B&H Academic, 2023); Anthony Hoekema's *Created in God's Image* (Grand Rapids: Eerdmans, 1994); or Charles Sherlock's *Doctrine of Humanity* (Downers Grove, IL: IVP Academic, 1997).

[6] R. Albert Mohler, *The Disappearance of God: Dangerous Beliefs in the New Spiritual Openness* (Colorado Springs: Multnomah, 2009), 48.

[7] Augustine, *Confessions*, trans. Henry Chadwick (London: Oxford University Press, 1992), 184.

and seen through the things that were made."[8] Thus, as the only beings created in God's image, our capacities to perceive, judge, and create beautiful things analogously reflect God as the archetype. Indeed, because we are imagers of God, "common grace endows all people . . . with a capacity for truth, goodness, beauty, and creativity."[9] As you can see from our top-down approach, all things in creation are derivative of God, and humanity's unique capacity to enjoy and cultivate beautiful things is an implication of being created in God's image (Gen 1:26–27).

Beauty as Human Artistry

In the garden of Eden, humans were given what is often referred to as a "cultural mandate" to care for and cultivate God's beautiful creation as his representatives over the earth (Gen 1:28; Ps 8:5–6). We must understand creation not only as a narrative of origin but also as a destiny. If not, we will miss the crucial point that creation is, in an important sense, unfinished.[10] Calvin Seerveld makes a compelling case for artistic creation as a proper response to God's call in Genesis for man to cultivate the earth to praise his name.[11] Seerveld argues, "The creation of God is unfinished, waiting historically to be used; its variegated meanings are waiting there to

---

[8] Augustine, *Confessions*, 184. Augustine is quoting Rom 1:20.

[9] Leland Ryken, *Culture in Christian Perspective*, ed. Frank Gaebelein (Portland, OR: Multnomah, 1986), 13.

[10] Jonathan King, *The Beauty of the Lord: Theology as Aesthetics* (Bellingham, WA: Lexham, 2018), 97.

[11] See Calvin Seerveld, *Rainbows for the Fallen World: Aesthetic Life and Artistic Task* (Toronto: Tuppence, 2005), 23–28.

be unleashed in a new chorus of praise for the Lord."[12] Just as God artfully and artistically designed and constructed all of creation, so humanity images God in its capacity for artful and creative development of all kinds; this is the aesthetic aspect of ruling and subduing.[13] This destiny is derivative of imaging God. It is an expression of humanity's calling to sub-creational participation as the continuation of God's purposes for the world. In later chapters, we will explore how we bear God's image in the world through our creative works, which mimic God's self-expression in creation.[14] For now, let us just say that man was fashioned by God as an aesthetic being in both form and function (Prov 8:30).

Aesthetic endeavors can be traced to the earliest parts of human civilization. Jubal, an early descendant of Adam, invented and played musical instruments (Gen 4:21). Even in the genealogy of Cain, early examples of music (and by extension the arts in general) along with farming and technology can be found (Gen 4:20–22). Bezalel's craftsmanship imitated God's construction of the cosmos, and psalmists like David and Moses composed and sang songs.[15] This is a point that Gene Edward Veith further develops by arguing that "every occupation . . . involves an art. Shoemakers, physicians, soldiers, merchants, rulers—all are artists in that they exercise their skills

---

[12] Seerveld, *Rainbows for the Fallen World*, 25.

[13] King, *The Beauty of the Lord*, 118

[14] See Steven B. Cowan and James S. Spiegel, *The Love of Wisdom: A Christian Introduction to Philosophy* (Nashville: B&H Academic, 2009), 428.

[15] Moses's songs can be found in Deuteronomy 32, Exodus 15, and Psalm 90.

creatively to make a product or perform a service for others."[16] This is an important corrective "to a common bias among historians, who tend to trace the development of the human race in terms of tools and weapons."[17] Aesthetic invention has played "a large part . . . in man's effort to build a meaningful world."[18] This sacred expression of human vocation is, according to Nicholas Wolterstorff, an act of "world projection" in which the artist mimics God's original creative act by fashioning a world for public appreciation and creates within the world for public use.[19] In mimicking God's creative act to express ourselves, we experience more fully the richness of being created in God's image.

Foundational to humanity's call to cultivate and create beautiful things is God's endorsement of such creation. According to Veith, "Clearly God, the ultimate Artist who created every detail of the universe purely from His own imagination, values the arts."[20] The use of aesthetic craftsmanship in the Exodus tabernacle illustrates not only the value of artistry but also that it is a gift from God (Exod 31:1–11; 35:30–36:2). In this passage, Bezalel is not only affirmed in his vocation as artist but also filled with the ability to fulfill his calling. In Exod 35:31, one reads, "He has filled him with God's Spirit, with wisdom, understanding, and ability in every kind of craft."

---

[16] Gene Edward Veith Jr., *State of the Arts: From Bezalel to Mapplethorpe* (Wheaton, IL: Crossway, 1991), 31.

[17] Ryken, *Culture in Christian Perspective,* 59.

[18] Lewis Mumford, *The Myth of the Machine: Technics and Human Development* (New York: Harcourt, Brace and World, 1966), 252.

[19] See Nicholas Wolterstorff, *Works and Worlds of Art* (Oxford, UK: Clarendon, 1980).

[20] Veith, *State of the Arts*, 25.

The tabernacle instructions in Exodus serve to illustrate God's value and investment in artists and their aesthetic endeavors. The abstract (nonrepresentational), representational, and symbolic art in both the tabernacle and the temple were ordained by God for aesthetic reasons.[21] Francis Schaeffer notes that "there was no pragmatic reason for the precious stones. They had no utilitarian purpose. God simply wanted beauty in the temple."[22] We do not build old covenant temples today, but it does not follow that our God cares little about beauty in corporate worship settings today. Beyond our buildings, this is especially the case when it comes to those who were created for worship. In many ways, Winston Churchill was correct in arguing that while we shape our buildings, our buildings also shape us.[23]

Beauty as Human Adornment

In a seminary course on Old Testament Hebrew, I distinctly remember my professor kneeling and sculpting imaginary clay to depict the biblical imagery encapsulated in the words of Gen 2:7, where God "formed" or "fashioned" the first human being from the dust. These are terms used to describe an artist's work, Adam being the crown of God's creative enterprise—his "masterpiece." Indeed, these Genesis passages paint the picture of God employing "particularly delicate artistic skills when He sculpted

[21] See Ryken, *Culture in Christian Perspective,* 54–57.

[22] Francis Schaeffer, *Art and the Bible* (Downers Grove, IL: IVP, 2006), 26.

[23] See Winston Churchill's speech to the House of Lords, October 28, 1943. Craig Bartholomew's work on "Place" in *Where Mortals Dwell* (Nashville: Baker Academic, 2011) is helpful here as well.

Adam and Eve from earthen materials."[24] Throughout the Bible, humans are physically described with aesthetic terms.[25] Unfortunately, speaking of a person's physical beauty can be a little thorny in our hypersexualized society; our imaginations are too often clouded with sensual longing. However, when we strive for purity in our acknowledgment of the beauty of others, we observe them not as *objects* of desire but as *subjects* created in God's image. This intentional distinction between "objects" and "subjects" speaks to the dignity of each person created in God's image and rightly indexes their beauty.

Even more, humans have long adorned their innate physical appearance with aesthetic embellishments as a way to enhance their beauty. A far cry from the fig leaf loincloths of post-fall Eden, Jacob designed and made a beautifully colored robe to adorn his beloved son Joseph (Gen 37:3). From the very beginning, cosmetics and clothing have been fashioned to enhance our aesthetic appeal (Gen 41:42; 45:22; Exod 26:36; 28:2; Isa 3:18–24; Rev 3:4). This is of particular interest when examining the sacred garments of Aaron, the high priest, which were made for glory and beauty (Exodus 28). It has been noted that the same colors, fabrics, and metals used for Aaron's garments were used for the tabernacle itself, signifying his consecration as holy unto God.[26] In this sense, "the tabernacle and

---

[24] Jo Ann Davidson, *Toward a Theology of Beauty: A Biblical Perspective* (Lanham, MD: University of America Press, 2008), 16.

[25] This holds true for both women (Gen 12:11; 24:16; 1 Sam 25:3; Song 1:15; 4:7) and men (Gen 39:6; 1 Sam 16:12; 2 Sam 14:25; Song 1:16; Dan 1:15).

[26] See J. A. Motyer, *The Message of Exodus: The Days of Our Pilgrimage*, The Bible Speaks Today, ed. J. A. Motyer and John Stott (Downers Grove, IL: InterVarsity, 2005), 269.

priesthood of Israel are the channels that God has chosen for his presence to break into the fallen world, and the aesthetic beauty of the tabernacle and priestly garments are meant to signify the sacredness of God's in-breaking glory."[27]

Beauty as Moral Adornment

In Scripture, the language of aesthetics and beauty is employed to speak not only of external embellishment but also of internal adornment. This becomes particularly clear in the New Testament where we are shown that beauty is much more than skin-deep. Consider the apostle Peter, who extols inward beauty above external ornamentation in 1 Pet 3:3–4: "Don't let your beauty consist of outward things like elaborate hairstyles and wearing gold jewelry or fine clothes, but rather what is inside the heart—the imperishable quality of a gentle and quiet spirit, which is of great worth in God's sight."[28]

As the church is called to be a royal priesthood, what was signified in Aaron's garments is realized in the moral adornment of all of God's New Testament people (1 Pet 2:9; Rev 1:6). Thus, character, as both moral piety and ethical resourcefulness, was ascribed to people as the beautiful adornment of godliness (Prov 31:10–31; 1 Tim 2:9–10; 1 Pet 3:3–5). Beauty, then, is related to our moral capacities and has implications on all human motivation, decision, and action. This moral aesthetic is a stark contrast to the religious elite of Jesus's day who appeared beautiful on the outside but were full of every kind

---

[27] John-Mark Hart, "Triune Beauty and the Ugly Cross: Towards a Theological Aesthetic," *Tyndale Bulletin* 66, no.2 (2015): 295.

[28] Paul exhorts women in a similar fashion in 1 Tim 2:9–10.

of inner impurity. Beauty has a moral trajectory and is often manifest in actions that are just, lawful, redemptive, and loving.[29] Spiritual formation is not simply the application of principles to our lives; it is rather the ever-increasing embodiment of beauty.[30] Hence, we must learn to see the aims of our growth in Christ not simply as responsibilities or commands but also as "experiments in a beautiful life."[31] This reality is rooted in God's essence and his desire for humanity because "the beauty of holiness" (Ps 29:2 NKJV) is first of all God's. As beings created in his image, our beautification is the progressive pursuit of his likeness.[32] There is a sense, then, that our creation in the "image of God" is not just something in us but is God's intention for us.[33] As Jonathan Edwards notes, "As God delights in His own beauty, He must necessarily delight in the creature's holiness; which is a conformity to and participation of it."[34]

---

[29] See Cowan and Spiegel, *The Love of Wisdom*, 445.

[30] I love how Nancy Leigh DeMoss articulates this: "To be holy is to be wholly satisfied with Christ. Above all, it is to reflect the beauty and the splendor of our holy Lord in this dark world. In pursuing holiness, you will fulfill and experience all that God had in mind when He created you." See Nancy Leigh DeMoss, *Holiness: The Heart God Purifies* (Chicago: Moody, 2008), 22.

[31] Evan B. Howard, "Formed into the Beauty of Christ: Reflections on Aesthetics and Christian Spiritual Formation," *Ogbomosho Journal of Theology* 16 (2011): 8.

[32] See C. E. B. Cranfield, *A Critical and Exegetical Commentary on the Epistle to the Romans*, vol. 1, ICC (London: T&T Clark, 1975), 432.

[33] This is the argument John F. Kilner makes in his *Dignity and Destiny: Humanity in the Image of God* (Grand Rapids: Eerdmans, 2015).

[34] Jonathan Edwards, *A Dissertation Concerning the End for Which God Created the World*, in *The Works of Jonathan Edwards, A.M.: With an Essay on His Genius and Writings, by Henry Rogers: And a Memoir by Sereno D. Wright*, ed. Henry Rogers, vol. 1 (London: W. Ball, 1839), 101.

In the New Testament letters, it is clear that conformity to the image of Christ is fundamental to our purpose as God's people (Gal 4:19; Heb 2:11). Intuitively, this makes sense because, as the incarnate image of God, Jesus is the archetypal image in which we are created.[35] Thus, Scripture gives us a script to follow as we endeavor to walk beautifully in a manner worthy of Christ, in a way that is befitting of the Lord (Col 1:10). A pursuit of the aesthetically adorned life is a means of maturing to the measure of Christ because our moral excellency is the proper reflection of his divine nature. While the purity of a beautiful life was lost in Eden, there remains a call to advance toward an ethical mode of being as the possibility of living such a life now actualized in the power of the Spirit.

As for our witness, a beautifully adorned life is the portal through which truth and goodness are not only seen but also loved and pursued. In this sense, there is a beautiful resonance of God's Word in the worshipful and obedient lives of those who conform to his Word to live a life that is aesthetically pleasing. For this reason, the apostle Paul urges believers to live in a manner that will make the teaching of the Lord beautiful and attractive before unbelievers (Titus 2:10). Interestingly enough, Paul uses the same word from Rom 1:20, which describes God's artistic work in creation, in reference to believers' being created for good works as God's workmanship (*poiēma*) in Eph 2:10. Because we are beings created in the image of God, beauty is a call to resemble, represent, and reflect God in the world not

---

[35] See Hammett and McCoy, *Humanity*, 82, or Oliver Crisp, "A Christological Model of the *Imago Dei*," in *Ashgate Research Companion to Theological Anthropology*, ed. Joshua R. Farris and Charles Taliaferro (New York: Routledge, 2016), 226.

only in adornment but also in artistry. We could argue that since beauty motivates virtue, it also requires virtue. Thus, the quality of our inner life is important in compelling us to act beautifully or to create that which is beautiful.[36]

Conclusion

Perhaps the most compelling witness to both inward and expressed beauty comes from the gospel account of the unnamed woman who anointed Jesus with expensive oil in a Bethany home.[37] When the fragrant aroma of her sacrifice filled the room, the disciples criticized her act as an extravagant waste. But Jesus quickly rebuked them, proclaiming that "she has done a beautiful thing to me" (Matt 26:10; Mark 14:6 NIV). Among other things, this narrative reminds us that "beauty is something done, a generous self-giving love for the other."[38] On one level, beauty is something to be offered to God. This unnamed woman offered back to God in adoration the very earthen materials he created, materials that had been

---

[36] In this sense, for the Christian, holiness is the state from which the most beautiful life and art arise as something inside that needs to get out.

[37] This story is found in Matt 26:6–14; Mark 14:3–9; and John 12:1–8. It is also used in many books exploring the interconnectivity of theology, beauty, and aesthetics. That should not surprise us. In bringing it into this book, I am simply doing my part in participating in Jesus's prophetic utterance that "wherever this gospel is proclaimed in the whole world, what this woman has done will also be told in memory of her" (Matt 26:13).

[38] Kevin J. Vanhoozer, *Pictures at a Theological Exhibition: Scenes of the Church's Worship, Witness, and Wisdom* (Downers Grove, IL: InterVarsity, 2016), 144.

fashioned by a cocreating craftsman. But the devotional act itself came from the overflow of a heart that had been beautified in the presence of Christ. In this sense, all our art and our aesthetically adorned lives can be presented to God as part of our worship, a "living sacrifice, holy and pleasing" (Rom 12:1) like fragrance before the Lord.

7

Further Up and Further In

Meadows, Museums, and Spiritual Formation

We don't just stand outside and analyze the natural world as a beam [of sunlight], but let the beam fall on our eyes of our heart, so that we see the source of the beauty—God himself. All of God's creation becomes a beam to be "looked along" or a sound to be "heard along" or a fragrance to be "smelled along" or a flavor to be "tasted along" or a touch to be "felt along." All of our senses become partners with the eyes of our hearts in perceiving the glory of God through the physical world.

—*John Piper*, When I Don't Desire God: How to Fight for Joy

Spiritual Formation as Being Attentive to Beauty

The question "How are you?" is often part of our typical greeting ritual. For many of us, it's simply an enquiry used to begin surface-level conversation or genuinely investigate the well-being of a friend. However, for the phenomenologist these words hold a much deeper meaning. (Phenomenology attends to the sensory dialogue between the subject and his or her setting, the setting being the object of consideration.) Those interested in the field of phenomenology seek a deeper or existential answer to this question, something along the lines of "How are you in this space?" This is a philosophical question related to embodied experience. For the thoughtful Christian, the question may be worded as, "In what ways are you aware of God's benevolent presence in your life?" Or "How are you experiencing God's created world in this moment?" The aim of asking this question in this particular way is to prompt an openness to or curiosity about the things around us. These phenomenological questions may seem too ethereal or abstract, perhaps even too mystical for those of us who exclusively attend to the one-sided rationalistic dimensions of our faith. However, this type of sensory attentiveness to the tacit or somatic can be surprisingly advantageous.

Oddly enough, this reality became clear to me when I was visiting the Metropolitan Museum of Art several years ago. We were only in New York for a weekend but spent much of an entire day lingering in front of the works of great artists like Caravaggio and Cassatt, Picasso and Pollock. One thing you may notice when visiting a museum is the peculiar absence of clocks on the wall. This is intentional, as it relates to how we purposely receive or experience what is around us. In a museum, you don't keep time because it is in these spaces that you are literally meant to be lost in it. Intuitively, when art connoisseurs stand before a Monet, they stop, settle, breathe, and contemplate. They behold. That is, they are "being held" by what is in front of them. Indeed, that day I distinctly remember losing track of time as I examined Van Gogh's brush strokes in the quietness of the gallery. It was as if the machinery of the clocks ceased in their production of seconds and minutes. It wasn't until we eventually exited the Met and made our way back into the "city that never sleeps" that the disparity between these two spaces, the museum and the city, became so "phenomenologically" jarring. The hurried footsteps of city dwellers, the traffic horns, and flashing advertisements reoriented us to the hurried pace of modernity. There was no time for contemplation. We were once again cogs in the machine, back in the "real world."

It's not unlike waking from a dream, as C. S. Lewis once said, when all your immediate frets and cares rush at you like wild animals. The question is, How can we "shove them back" and allow the "quieter life [to] come flowing in"?[1] So, how are you? What effect does beauty have in "how you are" in the world? More specifically related to our study, what role does aesthetics have in our contemplative spiritual formation? We could ask, Why have meadows been created or museums been curated?

---

[1] See C. S. Lewis, *Mere Christianity* (New York: HarperOne, 1980), 196.

The Experience of Beauty and Human Embodiment

Our rich Christian tradition has built within it a conviction that "God has made us embodied, sensory beings in a world that is teeming with holy and delightful sights, sounds, smells, and tastes that are among those good gifts descending from above for which we should give thanks."[2] The word *embodiment* is important here and is defined by our "perceptual experience or our mode of presence and engagement in the world."[3] This involves our "sensing," that is, an act of understanding or "making sense" of our experiences. As we explore spiritual formation in light of what it means to be embodied beings, it is helpful to note the Enlightenment dichotomy between the "immaterial and material," or the "rational and experiential," a separation that has cast a shadow over these discussions for centuries.[4] Philosopher Charles Taylor has gone so far as to argue that modern Christianity has experienced an "excarnation," that is "a transfer out of embodied forms of religious life, to those which are more 'in the head.'"[5] However, "a central conviction of Christian faith" is "that the transcendent God became incarnate, en-fleshed in Jesus of Nazareth."[6] The

[2] John-Mark Hart, "Triune Beauty and the Ugly Cross: Towards a Theological Aesthetic," *Tyndale Bulletin* 66, no. 2 (2015): 305.

[3] See Gregg R. Allison, *Created in the Image of God: Applications and Implications for Our Cultural Confusion,* ed. David S. Dockery with Lauren McAfee (Nashville: Forefront Books, 2023), 107.

[4] The enlightenment championed a triumph of rationality and, with it, an estrangement between faith and reason.

[5] Charles Taylor, *A Secular Age* (Cambridge, MA: Harvard University Press, 2007), 554.

[6] Benjamin P. Myers, *A Poetics of Orthodoxy: Christian Truth as Aesthetic Foundation* (Eugene, OR: Wipf and Stock, 2020), 15.

Christian emphasis on embodiment finds its "pinnacle in the incarnation of the second person of the Trinity," as God the Son took on flesh, sinew, and bone.[7] Taylor's charge of "excarnation" regarding the modern church is a decisive "move of disembodiment and abstraction," a break from the particularities of embodiment and communion.[8] Thus, we should return to the notion that spirituality involves the whole person. After all, the spiritual and physical are inextricably mingled (Mark 12:30). Formation of one's spiritual life, then, does not happen solely within the realm of the mind but also includes the body and senses. This is why James K. A. Smith often reminds us that we are more than "brains on a stick."[9] This is not to say that one should neglect the life of the mind, not at all. There is always the not-so-subtle danger of subjectivism that can lose sight of God, who is there and has revealed himself to us as rational beings. However, as Makoto Fujimura has noted following the project of enlightenment, "Christians have many propositions

[7] Myers, 21.

[8] James K. A. Smith, *How (Not) to Be Secular: Reading Charles Taylor* (Grand Rapids: Eerdmans, 2014), 58.

[9] James K. A. Smith, *You Are What You Love: The Spiritual Power of Habit* (Grand Rapids: Brazos, 2014), 3. Smith would also argue that the modern church has fallen prey to the intellectualism of modernity, thus underestimating the importance of the embodied experience of beauty and its place in holistic spiritual formation. Again, Smith reasons that humanity's being-in-the-world is more aesthetic and deductive. Therefore, neglecting beauty among the transcendentals flattens one's perception of God's creation as a disenchanted space, numbing one to the formative power of the aesthetic experience. Since beauty expresses evidence for truth and goodness by way of experiential proof, Christians must learn to be epistemological optimists. See James K. A. Smith, *Imagining the Kingdom: How Worship Works* (Grand Rapids: Baker Academic, 2013), 31–41, 108.

about what Christianity is that are often based upon an analytical approach to understanding truth as a set of propositional beliefs, such that understanding and explaining take dominance over experiencing and intuiting."[10]

There is a real sense in which experiencing beauty is a type of knowing. Indeed, the experience of beauty does not exclude analytical modes of knowing. To experience beauty is to know experientially what would otherwise only be known abstractly or in theory. Of the transcendentals (truth, goodness, and beauty), Brendan Thomas Sammon argues that beauty communicates truth and goodness with a greater capacity to engage the whole person than mere data or information can. In many cases, "no knowledge can come about unless the known is first desired as something to be known": indeed, "beauty ensures such a condition. In other words, beauty is that in a given thing which allows it to attract interest."[11]

Take, for example, the musician who first fell in love with the classical genre at an early age. After years of training, he or she can listen to a piece by Mozart and systematically identify its structure, melody, and pitch. That person can "know" the organizational particularities of the piece. As a lifelong enthusiast, he or she can also bask in the experience of the beautiful dynamics of the piece as a whole. This is a type of knowing. Or consider the astrophysicist who understands the details of the active ingredients of cosmic nurseries through the study of radio, optical, and infrared telescopes but who also remains

[10] Makoto Fujimura, *Art + Faith: A Theology of Making* (Cambridge, MA: Yale University Press, 2021), 4.

[11] Brendan Thomas Sammon, *Called to Attraction: An Introduction to the Theology of Beauty* (Eugene, OR: Wipf and Stock, 2017), 13, 16.

wonderstruck when taking in the transcendent beauty of the night sky with the naked eye. Both "knowing" the particularities and "experiencing" the whole are not at odds. In fact, both serve as reminders that the aesthetic beauty of created things is a signpost that draws us toward the divine. However, we are often wary of aesthetic experiences. How often have we heard, "Don't trust your feelings or intuitions"? As if they have nothing to offer at all. What if, because we are embodied beings, God has spiritual aims for the enchantment we often experience within his created world? What would it take for our eyes to be opened to take in every aesthetic experience as blossoming with deeper meaning? This is where the concept of spiritual formation is helpful for "how we are in the world." Spiritual formation is more of a cumulative term, as it encompasses all the experiences that could shape one's religious sensibilities and awareness. To put it another way, spiritual formation leans on not only the cognitive but also the affective capacities that enable humanity to participate in God. But what do I mean by participating *in* God?

Spiritual Formation as Participation in Our Beautiful God

Many years ago, my friend group of young professionals would occasionally spend a weekend night exploring the downtown streets of our city. One evening after curiously entering a bohemian shop, we all found ourselves on a patio on the fringes of a drum circle enclosing free-spirited dancers. I remember being somewhat amused and awestruck by the whole scene, caught up in the beauty of the moment. I was drawn to how everyone inside the circle exuded joy. Everyone participating radiated that special intensity that could only come from submitting oneself to the tempo of the whole. It was only when one of the singing drummers motioned for us to enter the dance or pick up an instrument that we became aware, in a phenomenological sense, of the choice before us. You see, to become enveloped in the circle was to consent to the others, to enter the rhythmic dynamic that began before we arrived. As I look back on this moment, I cannot help but be reminded of the all-too-familiar illustration C. S. Lewis uses to depict the movement of life in God, the image of a "divine dance."[12] As we move deeper into spiritual formation, this illustration can be helpful to guide us into what it means to participate in our triune God. Let me explain in two parts.

First, the Christian doctrine of the Trinity espouses that God is one, existing eternally in three persons: Father, Son, and Holy Spirit. The revelation that God is Trinity—three persons in one nature—understands them as existing one for the other but in perfect communion. A proper doctrine of the Trinity acknowledges three persons who are inseparable. Without dividing the divine unity, we would say that the real distinction of the persons resides in the relationships that relate them to one another. The source of beauty that proceeds from the Holy Spirit is the bond of love between the Father and the Son and undeniably is beautiful itself. In this beauty, the Father reveals the Son, the Son reveals the Father, and the Father and the Son are revealed

---

[12] C. S. Lewis, *Mere Christianity*, 136. Timothy Keller uses the same illustration in *The Reason for God*, describing the "dance of God." See *The Reason for God: Belief in an Age of Skepticism* (New York: Penguin, 2009), 214–21.

by the Holy Spirit. This is the divine eternal life in procession. In short, beauty names the triune dance of God's eternal delight in God's own glory.[13]

Among other things, this means that God is, in essence, relational. The inner life of the triune God can be characterized by mutually self-giving love, a mirrored rejoicing in the glory of one another.[14] This is what Cornelius Plantinga describes as a trinitarian "movement of overture" where the Father, Son, and Spirit "envelop and encircle" one another in beautiful delight.[15] What, then, do we make of beauty in our world? As we have seen, creation exists not only as derivative of the triune God but also as overflow of trinitarian delight. As Jonathan Edwards reminds us, "All beauty to be found throughout the whole creation is but the reflection of the diffused beams of the Being who hath an infinite fullness and brightness of glory."[16] Thus, all properties of aesthetics are secondary and analogical to the true, spiritual, primary beauty found in God.

---

[13] See David Bentley Hart, *The Beauty of the Infinite: The Aesthetics of Christian Truth* (Grand Rapids: Eerdmans, 2004), 155–78; Fred Sanders, *The Deep Things of God: How the Trinity Changes Everything* (Wheaton, IL: Crossway, 2017), 61–96; John Piper, *The Pleasures of God: Meditations on God's Delight in Being God* (Colorado Springs: Multnomah, 2000), 25–46.

[14] At certain times in church history, the Greek word *perichoresis* (rotation or circumincession) was used to refer to the relationship of the three persons of the triune God (Father, Son, and Holy Spirit) to one another as well as to the mutual indwelling of the persons of the Trinity, as in John's Gospel account, "I am in the Father and the Father is in me" (John 14:11). See also John 1:18; 16:14; 17:4–5.

[15] Cornelius Plantinga, *Engaging God's World: A Christian Vision of Faith, Learning, and Living* (Grand Rapids: Eerdmans, 2002), 41.

[16] Jonathan Edwards, *The Works of Jonathan Edwards*, vol. 8 (New Haven, CT: Yale University Press, 1992), 550–51.

Second, following Augustine, one way to understand the "image of God" is as *carpax Dei* (capable of participation with God), that is in "relation to Him by whom [His "image"] is impressed."[17] We have already explored the *imago Dei* as concepts of resemblance, representation, and reflection. However, according to Augustine's model, we could argue that being "image bearers" is first a relational quality and then is secondarily reflected in our attributes and capacities.[18] As we have seen above, the relational quality imbedded in the *imago Dei* is derivative of the inner relational dynamic of our triune God. Brian Rosner explains this relational dynamic of our created constitution in his work *Known by God: A Biblical Theology of Personal Identity*. For Rosner, grounding these discussions about humanity in identity allows us to acknowledge our functions and attributes without reducing our doctrine of humanity to these capacities, functions, and attributes alone.[19] In other words, we come to understand ourselves in God, and we come

---

[17] Augustine, *On the Trinity* 12.11.16, in *The Nicene and Post-Nicene Fathers*, ed. Alexander Roberts et al. (Peabody, MA: Hendrickson, 1979), 3:161.

[18] See Jason McMartin, "The Theandric Union as Imago Dei and Capax Dei," in *Christology: Ancient and Modern*, ed. Oliver Crisp and Fred Sanders (Grand Rapids: Zondervan, 2013), 137.

[19] Brian Rosner, *Known by God: A Biblical Theology of Personal Identity* (Grand Rapids: Zondervan, 2017). See also John S. Hammett and Katie J. McCoy, *Humanity*, Theology for the People of God, ed. David S. Dockery, Nathan A. Finn, and Christopher W. Morgan (Brentwood, TN: B&H Academic, 2023), 108. Marc Cortez notes that an anthropological model that only focuses on capacities, functions, and attributes runs the risk of excluding certain human beings. See *Theological Anthropology: A Guide for the Perplexed* (London: T&T Clark, 2010), 20.

to understand everything about ourselves in relation to God. Furthermore, as beings created in God's image, we are fundamentally oriented toward God. Thus, to commune with and participate in God is to fulfill the intent and meaning of being human. Even when we speak of God as Creator, it is a description of a relationship that befalls creatures.[20] In other words, we understand creation not just as a temporal act (as in "God created") but as a relation between God and all that he has brought forth by the power of his word.

Spiritual Formation as Consent

Understanding this type of intermingled relationship among Creator, creatures, and creation requires what theologians have termed "mutual consent"—that is, the relationship between the giver and/or object to the beholder in which the subject may enter and participate.[21] Following divine revelation, by which God discloses himself and his beauty, the second movement of beauty for the subject is upward, by which he or she responds to the God who has made himself known.[22] It is mutual moving of the recipient to the object, and the object (in this case, God) moving toward the recipient. After all, even secondary experiences of beauty in creation involve consenting. When something

---

[20] Peter J. Leithart explores this in *Creator: A Theological Interpretation of Genesis 1* (Downers Grove, IL: IVP, 2023).

[21] See Roland Delattre, *Beauty and Sensibility in the Thought of Jonathan Edwards* (Eugene, OR: Wipf and Stock, 2006), 22.

[22] Aquinas also develops his theory around similar movements. The progression begins when one is struck by beauty then is drawn in toward that beauty; delight is experienced as one rests in what is beheld (Thomas Aquinas, *Summa Theologiae*, I q. 5 a. 4 ad 1).

appears beautiful to a person, that individual is compelled to submit to the presence of that beauty. As Jonathan Edwards put it, "One alone, without any reference to any more, cannot be excellent; for in such case there can be no manner of relation no way, and therefore no such thing as consent. Indeed what we call One, may be excellent because of a consent of parts, or some consent of those in that being, that are distinguished into a plurality in some way or other. But in a being that is absolutely without any plurality, there cannot be excellency, for there can be no such thing as consent or agreement."[23] Furthermore, the more fullness of beauty a thing has, the greater one's pleasure or delight will be toward that beauty—thus returning us to our triune God, who is the source and substance of true beauty. In the words of Thomas Aquinas, "The beauty of the creature is nothing other than the similitude of divine beauty participated in things."[24]

We cannot behold God apart from revelation through Jesus Christ. Christ is the cornerstone not only of the Christian faith but also of the worldview that accompanies it. This Christocentric progression was important for Hans Urs von Balthasar, who held that the act of perceiving revelation cannot be separated from the enrapturing form of God's beauty in the person of Jesus, through whom we are drawn toward the divine life.[25] As John Navone has said, "The Father has given us

---

[23] Jonathan Edwards, *The Works of Jonathan Edwards*, vol. 1 (Carlisle, PA: The Banner of Truth Trust, 1995), ccxxix.

[24] Thomas Aquinas, *Commentary on the Divine Names*, chap. 4, lecture 5, quoted in Sammon, *Called to Attraction*, 97.

[25] See Hans Urs von Balthasar, *The Glory of the Lord: A Theological Aesthetics* (San Francisco: Ignatius, 2009), 92–94.

the Son and Spirit that we might share the triune God's eternal happiness."[26] Thus God journeys from himself toward his people in Christ, making it possible for the Christian to journey away from self toward God.[27] Our communion with the triune God is a gift of grace: through faith we receive in Christ and through the Spirit we become receptive of all that God is and all that God has given.[28] John Owen argues that our communion with God consists of "communication of himself unto us, with our return unto him of that which he requires and accepts."[29] In this sense, we participate in God through enjoyment and praise that is "rejoicing." This mode of participation understands creation, and all the beauty within it, as something coming from the Creator (who is beautiful in himself) to be consented to through faith in Christ.[30]

The gospel, then, is divine hospitality. In Christ, we are invited into the circle of trinitarian reciprocal delight, as it were, to both peer into with awe and participate in praise.[31] It is only after seeing from inside the circle that we "come to our senses" and understand that we are being invited into something that

---

[26] John Navone, *Toward a Theology of Beauty* (Collegeville, PA: Liturgical, 2009), 29.

[27] Balthasar, *The Glory of the Lord*, 125.

[28] Interesting to note on this point, in the second book in his treatise *On the Trinity*, Hilary of Poitiers attributed "eternity" to the Father, "beauty" to the Son, and "enjoyment" to the Holy Spirit.

[29] John Owen, *Communion with the Triune God*, ed. Kelly M. Kapic and Justin Taylor (Wheaton, IL: Crossway, 2007), 94.

[30] I would commend Andrew Davison's *Participation in God: A Study in Christian Doctrine and Metaphysics* (Cambridge, UK: Cambridge University Press, 2020), in which Davison offers an unprecedented study on the idea of "participation."

[31] See David Bentley Hart, *The Beauty of the Infinite*, 155.

has preceded us. The beautiful life of God not only is all around us but also comes to us most directly through the person of Jesus Christ in the Spirit. W. David O. Taylor explains, "The triune God is already active in creation. In Christ, the physical, affective, imaginative, and metaphoric aspects of our humanity are already being transformed. The Father is already liberating the cosmos from its bondage to decay. The Spirit is already enabling the stuff of heaven and earth to resound with the glory of God."[32]

The gospel does not just affect the way we think; it changes the way we experience the world.[33] When we consider creation not only as the existing derivative of God but also as the overflow of trinitarian delight, we begin to understand what Jonathan Edwards meant in writing, "The beauty of the world consists wholly of sweet mutual consents, either within itself or with the supreme being. As to the corporeal [physical] world, though there are many other sorts of consents, yet the sweetest and most charming beauty of it is its resemblance of spiritual beauties."[34]

All too often in our everyday interaction with the world, the objects of aesthetic experience come before us as either "to be known" technically or "to be used" in the utilitarian sense. But there is another posture open to us in which "appearances are ordered as objects to be contemplated. . . . to put it another

---

[32] W. David O. Taylor, *Glimpses of the New Creation: Worship and the Formative Power of the Arts* (Grand Rapids: Eerdmans, 2019), 9–10.

[33] Again, I am conceiving aesthetic experience within the realms of cognitive thought and the appetite of desire.

[34] Jonathan Edwards, *Images or Shadows of Divine Things* (Westport, CT: Greenwood, 1948), 135.

way: we savor the world, as something given."[35] We could argue, then, that the beauty found in our world functions as spiritual "smelling salts," for beauty wakes us up to the reality that, as the poet Gerard Manley Hopkins reminds us, "The world is charged with the grandeur of God."[36]

Beauty and Biblical Discernment

Perhaps your theological senses are rising in defense at this point in this chapter's argument. After all, couldn't the beauties of this world lead us into a delight that also imprisons and destroys us if our affections are not centered on the God of beauty? This can certainly be the case. Augustine is a suitable teacher in this matter as he was cognizant of just how easy it is to become distracted and immersed in the signs of beauty or aesthetic experiences themselves. In *Confessions*, Augustine famously repents of being consumed with lesser beauties, which distracted him from the most beautiful God:

> Late I have loved You, Beauty so ancient and so new, late have I loved You! And behold, You were within me, and I was outside, and I sought you there, and threw myself deformed, upon the beautiful things You made. You were with me; but I was not with you. Those things held me far from You; things which would not even exist

[35] Roger Scruton, *The Soul of the World* (Princeton, NJ: Princeton University Press, 2014), 136. But this does not mean that they have no utility whatsoever.

[36] Gerard Manley Hopkins, "God's Grandeur," in Bernard W. Kelly, *The Mind and Poetry of Gerard Manley Hopkins* (New York: Haskell House, 1971), 5.

> unless they were in You. You called and cried out and broke upon my deafness; You shone forth and glowed and chased away my blindness; You blew fragrantly on me, and I drew breath and I pant for You; I tasted You, and I hunger and thirst for You; You touched me, and I was inflamed with desire for your peace.[37]

Augustine's conversion was prompted by hearing a child's voice declare *Tolle, lege* ("take up and read"), at which point he opened Paul's letter to the Romans, only to be warned of exchanging "ultimate delight for penultimate satisfaction."[38] Something must be said about the task of biblical discernment when experiencing and evaluating beauty. If beauty and aesthetics are understood as secondary, as a reflection of the primary beauty of God, then one must avoid the idolatrous pull that often accompanies these experiences. Jonathan Edwards was correct when articulating that "it is all deformity and darkness in comparison of the brighter glories and beauties of the Creator of all."[39] In this sense, when one delights in any earthly beauty, whether it be in the meadow or the museum, one is only seeing emanations that come from the God of all beauty.[40]

Thus, Christians must learn to properly index and at the same time move beyond the beauty of lesser objects toward the One who is beautiful, namely, God. Concerning proper

---

[37] Augustine, *Confessions*, X, 27, 38.

[38] James Fodor, *The Beauty of God: Theology and the Arts* (Downers Grove, IL: InterVarsity, 2007), 166.

[39] Jonathan Edwards, *The Works of Jonathan Edwards*, vol. 10 (New Haven, CT: Yale University Press, 1992), 421.

[40] See Jonathan Edwards, *The Works of Jonathan Edwards*, vol. 13 (New Haven, CT: Yale University Press, 1992), 278–80.

discernment, one comes to understand that unless the affections are grounded in biblical realities, they are spurious and ungenuine and will quickly lose their moorings.[41] Without the discernment given by Scripture, the power and attraction of lesser beauties often become a barrier to pointing beyond themselves.[42] Setting things in their "proper colors" denotes grounding one's discernment in biblical categories to understand and judge beauty and aesthetic experiences. To use the words of Dorothy Sayers, Christians must "commit" to biblical revelation in discovering "the nature of all truth," and in this particular case, the nature of truth concerning beauty and aesthetics.[43]

The reflective reader of Scripture will understand that, within the Bible, there is extensive vocabulary given for expressing the concept of beauty. Modern English translations provide around one hundred biblical references to the experience of beauty or aesthetic pleasure.[44] The biblical

---

[41] See Samuel Logan's comments on the phenomenology in *The Preacher and Preaching: Reviving the Art*, ed. Samuel T. Logan Jr. (Phillipsburg, NJ: P&R, 1986), 129–60.

[42] It would be wise to heed and apply Edward's wisdom on this point as it relates to spiritual formation; the aim should be "to stir up the pure minds of the saints, and quicken their affections, by often bringing the great things of religion to their remembrance, and setting them before them in their proper colors." Jonathan Edwards, *A Treatise Concerning Religious Affections* (New York: Leavitt, Trow, 1845), 16.

[43] See Dorothy Sayers, *The Whimsical Christian* (New York: Macmillan, 1978), 74.

[44] The Old Testament presents a Hebrew aesthetic vocabulary built from at least fourteen verbal roots, while the New Testament provides six Greek words. For one of the most extensive modern treatments on the use of the term *beauty* in the Bible, see Jo Ann Davidson's *Toward a Theology of Beauty* (Lanham, MD: University Press of America, 2008).

writers used a rich glossary for the aesthetic, with a network of meanings that encompassed ideas of spiritual, physical, and artistic beauty.[45] Throughout the Bible, the language of beauty is applied to God, to artifacts, to people, and to nature (*artifacts*: Josh 7:21; Ps 48:2; Isa 5:9; 28:5; 52:1; 62:3; Lam 2:15; Ezek 7:20; 16:12; 23:42; 33:32; Rom 9:21; *people*: Gen 12:11; 1 Sam 25:3; 2 Sam 14:25; Prov 20:29; Song 1:15–16; Isa 44:13; Acts 7:20; Heb 11:23; *nature*: Gen 2:9; Ps 19:1; Song 2:12–13; 7:13; Isa 28:1, 4; 40:6; Hos 14:6; Matt 6:28–29; Jas 1:11).

As we attend to reflective reading of Scripture, we are given an "ecosystem of metaphors and a garden of words."[46] This is why artists "have always been particularly attracted to the books of poetry and wisdom and prophecy in the Bible because there they meet people of like mind."[47] However, our modern impulses often lead us, as Malcolm Guite notes, to treat Scripture "as though it were some kind of literalistic science manual."[48] When given to this paradigm, we often miss the aesthetic nature of Scripture and how it enriches one's understanding of beauty. Indeed, the Bible is undergirded by its own aesthetic manifestation as a significant work of art abounding with artistic beauty through its literary form. Leland Ryken argues that if beauty and aesthetics were of no consequence in the biblical text, then

---

[45] See Francis M. DuBose, *God Who Sends: A Fresh Quest for Biblical Mission* (Nashville: Broadman, 1983), 92. See also Davidson, *Toward a Theology of Beauty*, 151–71.

[46] Makoto Fujimura, *Art + Faith*, 37.

[47] Steve Turner, *Imagine: A Vision for Christians in the Arts* (Downers Grove, IL: InterVarsity, 2017), 89.

[48] See Malcolm Guite, *Lifting the Veil: Imagination and the Kingdom of God* (London: Canterbury, 2022), 15.

"there would have been no good reason for biblical poets to put their utterances into intricately patterned verse form, or for biblical storytellers to compose masterfully compact and carefully designed stories."[49]

The aesthetic dimension of Scripture is by no means negligible; after all, the biblical writers have written with an aesthetic dimension in mind and, in doing so, have enriched our understanding of the world through their aesthetically crafted vocabulary.[50] The aesthetic nature of Scripture has a depth that grips and haunts us, is ever open to us; and when we give ourselves to attentive reflection, every glance begins to see the world with fresh eyes. We might even say that every biblical text has a poetic dimension to it because language itself is poetic. Paying attention to the poetic nature of Scripture means attending to the words, the words in their context, and the overtones of those words as they are echoed throughout the entire canon. Thus, we must read with all the senses on alert. Peter J. Leithart illustrates this by pointing out that musicians and composers submit to the authoritative material in the composition of a piece as it has been given from the hand of its author but play it freely within limitations.[51] The point is, the more we attend to the Scripture as discipline for our delight, the more we are trained to see the beauty within creation blossoming with deeper meaning.

---

[49] Leland Ryken, *The Christian Imagination: The Practice of Faith in Literature and Writing* (Colorado Springs: WaterBrook, 2002), 26.

[50] Davidson, *Toward a Theology of Beauty*, 151. Also, see Frank Burch Brown, *Religious Aesthetics* (Princeton, NJ: Princeton University Press, 1989), 40–41.

[51] See Peter J. Leithart's *Theopolitan Reading* (Monroe, LA: Athanasius, 2020), specifically on "spiritual reading" (pp. 1–24).

Seeing as Shaping

In an interview, Jeremy Begbie once used Bach's *Goldberg Variations* as an example of how a simple chord progression developed in thirty variations allows one to hear more and more with each layer. The genius of Bach's piece is that after an hour or so, after all "variations," the beginning of the aria is played again. However, one cannot hear the end "apart from the memory of the extraordinary things Bach has shown us" through its entirety. Begbie adds, "In other words, now we hear this aria not simply as a replication of what we heard before; we hear it as varied, replete with diversity. It has gathered to itself a richness, a huge variety of moods and colors. Bach makes us hear more in what we hear, so to speak."[52] There is a sense in which *every* aesthetic experience strikes the same chord. It is a reminder that the beauty in this world beckons us to God, who is the source and substance of all true beauty. As we read the "book of the world" through the "book of the Word," to use the words of Irish poet Seamus Heaney, we begin to hear the "music [we] would never have known to listen for."[53] What then of the creation of meadows and the curation of museums?

The excessive surplus of beauty in our world is not gratuitous but has an attractive—even sanctifying—power. Following Thomas Aquinas, we would posit not only that aesthetic experiences provide humanity with a glimpse of our transcendent God, making us aware of his presence, but also that aesthetic

[52] Kathleen Housely, "A Conversation with Jeremy Begbie," *Image Journal* 85 (summer 2015), https://imagejournal.org/article/a-conversation-with-jeremy-begbie/.

[53] Seamus Heaney, "The Rainstick," *New Republic*, August 30, 1993, https://newrepublic.com/article/114546/seamus-heaney-rainstick.

longing can serve as a path that draws us toward him.[54] Beauty can penetrate to the very depths of one's heart, stilling it in ways nothing else can. Thus, the allure of beauty is more than a fleeting experience. It calls us beyond itself. It shapes who we become and how we are related to the world, others, and God.[55] Indeed, according to Jonathan Edwards, the sanctification of a believer was the most significant aspect of our participation in beauty.[56] This is why sanctification is sometimes called a believer's "beautification." Beauty is formative, as it shapes the mind through progressions of thought and expands perception through experience, in turn blossoming into an appreciation for God's creation and a love of the Creator.[57] Thus, beauty and aesthetics serve as effective servants to our spiritual formation, making us aware of God's presence in our world and in our lives.

Conclusion

God has made everything beautiful in its time to be beheld (see Eccl 3:11). God made us to "be held" by beauty because aesthetic awareness is an integral aspect of who we are. We have been created as embodied beings for communion with our triune God, in both cognitive and affective capacities. Through Christ, we are invited to step into the circle of the divine life

[54] Thomas Aquinas, *De veritate* 2, 1, ad 9m.

[55] See Sammon, *Called to Attraction*, 54–56.

[56] See Alan Heimert, *Religion and the American Mind* (Cambridge, MA: Harvard University Press, 1966), 194.

[57] See Charles Arand and Erik Herrmann's excellent essay "Attending to the Beauty of Creation and New Creation," in *Concordia Pages*, April 10, 2019, https://scholar.csl.edu/cgi/viewcontent.cgi?article=1004&context=concordiapages.

and participate in praise. This is God's intent for "how we are" in this world as a mode of presence and engagement. This is how God continues to form us like clay. With this perspective, we can pass through this world and enjoy all that it has to offer, while realizing that the final delight of being in God's presence will overwhelm anything this world can offer. Thus, "the world is neither so full of evil that we can't enjoy it nor so full of goodness that we can abandon ourselves to it."[58] We receive what beauty the world offers in direct proportion to the way we give ourselves to attentiveness or consent to what God has offered. The call of spiritual formation is to *open our eyes* or to *come to our senses*. For if the "aesthetic life is malfunctioning or undeveloped . . . then that human life misses a notch . . . has bare spots, or possibly suffers deformity."[59]

---

[58] Turner, *Imagine*, 86.

[59] Calvin Seerveld, *Rainbows for the Fallen World: Aesthetic Life and Artistic Task* (Toronto: Tuppence, 2005), 49–50.

8

A Glimmer of Transcendence

On Artisans, Art, and Appreciation

Art enables us to find ourselves and lose ourselves at the same time. The mind that responds to the intellectual and spiritual values that lie hidden in a poem, a painting, or a piece of music, discovers a spiritual vitality that lifts it above itself, takes it out of itself, and makes it present to itself on a level of being that it did not know it could ever achieve.

—*Thomas Merton,* No Man Is an Island

Art as an Invitation

Andrew Wyeth is widely regarded as one of America's most treasured realist painters in the twentieth century. Wyeth had an uncanny ability to capture the solemn nostalgia of rural American life with painstakingly controlled brushstrokes and a muted color palette. In one of his most intriguing and iconic paintings,

Christina's World (1948), a brunette woman is depicted lying in a grassy field with her left hand reaching toward a far-off farmhouse. The painting is modeled after Wyeth's neighbor and muse, Anna Olson. It is believed that Olson suffered from a degenerative muscular disorder that limited her to crawling around her house and family land. There is nothing flashy or wildly fantastic about the subject matter of *Christina's World*, yet this painting has a distinctly powerful effect on the onlooker. Even without our knowing the context, the piece is commanding enough to draw us in and prompt contemplative questions. "Is she calling for help, calling for someone off in the distance?" "Why is she lying there alone or dragging her body around the property?" If we linger before the painting long enough, we will find ourselves wanting to join Christina in her uphill struggle as she longingly reaches for her home.

When asked why he chose Christina as a subject to be painted, Wyeth explained that he wanted to capture the "strength and poetry of her will" to "make the viewer sense that her world may be limited physically but by no means spiritually."[1] Great works of art like *Christina's World* remind us that, as Ryan Duns argues, there is a "surplus of meaning behind a text" that "invites us into ongoing engagement."[2] Art invites interpretation and

---

[1] "Andrew Wyeth, *Christina's* World," the website of the Museum of Modern Art, https://www.moma.org/audio/playlist/172/2279. In this interview, Wyeth was prompted to defend why he chose to paint his disabled neighbor in the first place, as some found it controversial. To which Wyeth explained that he chose this subject matter "to do justice to her extraordinary conquest of a life that for many would be desolate."

[2] Ryan G. Duns, SJ, *Spiritual Exercises for a Secular Age: Desmond and the Quest for God* (Notre Dame, IN: University of Notre Dame Press, 2020), 203.

requires contemplation. One of the great wonders of art is not simply the deep experience it imparts, but that there is an artist behind it who creates and incites this exchange for us. To put it another way, there is a reason for the awestruck gasp provoked by standing in the Florence basilica taking in Volterrano's frescoed ceiling and declaring, "I can't believe a human did that!"

Art as Co-creational Participation

It has been said that a famous sculptor was asked how he approached his work, to which he responded with something along the lines of, "I see a masterpiece in the marble, and I chip away at the block until I set it free, and do so for everyone else to see." Beauty is meant to be shared. From a distinctly Christian perspective, art reminds us that all creative acts overflow from our image-bearing capacity as human beings. When we create art, we are imitating our creating and communicating God. Even more, as we express ourselves in making, we begin to fully experience the richness of being created in the *imago Dei*. Our artistic endeavors are derivative of God just as all secondary beauty is derivative of God's unmatched beauty. Yet while God created all things "out of nothing," requiring no preexisting material, we work with the materials God has given. In this sense, we are "co-creators." Indeed, every act of creative making is to be a worshipful response to offer back to God what has been given to us.

God's commission to Adam and Eve is a reminder that creation is unfinished, awaiting humanity's co-creational participation. The word *commission* is not unimportant here, as it speaks to the "co-mission" imbedded in our call as humans to exercise dominion over the earth. The call to create is seen from the earliest pages of Genesis, where Adam is assigned the task of naming the animals (Gen 2:19–20). In creating names for each kind of beast and bird, Adam separates and dignifies each animal and, in doing so, affirms their distinct belonging in our world.[3] Remarkably, God has invited humanity into the process of making the world a fitting place through harnessing earthen materials for aesthetic purposes. And as Makoto Fujimura reminds us, beautiful art is "created as objects of contemplation, and thus cannot be brought forth without consideration of the persons who are to contemplate them."[4] Art is an act of human communication, by which one expresses ideas and conveys emotions. Art addresses ideas, values, and perceptions. Just as God has revealed himself in creation, when we mimic God's creative act, we imbed our unique presence into every work of art. It is in God's self-giving nature to create out of love; so, too, is it to be with humans. Thus, all art is a way of helping others know, understand, and utilize our world for God's glory. It is a type of sharing, of giving for our neighbor's good. How, then, does art function in this way?

Art as Confrontational Parable

I've often thought of art as a kind of parable. Parables are told to point the listener to something else, much like all secondary beauty is analogical to the primary beauty found in God. Consider Jesus's use of parables as artistic storytelling and note that the recipient is situated to stand in between the world of the story

---

[3] See Russ Ramsey, *Rembrandt Is in the Wind: Learning to Love Art through the Eyes of Faith* (Grand Rapids: Zondervan, 2022), 7; Makoto Fujimura, *Art + Faith: A Theology of Making* (Cambridge, MA: Yale University Press, 2021), 95–100.

[4] Fujimura, *Art + Faith*, 82.

and their own world in contemplative comparison. This is why we often speak of "entering the world" of a story as a way of allowing its narrative to shape us. But like art, parables are not always obvious or self-explanatory. Thus, parables place the burden of responsibility on its listeners by forcing them to wrestle with a message that is both being revealed and concealed. There is always more than meets the eye, provoking a deeper sense of wonder that carries the recipient beyond that which appears on the surface, so the only way to truly understand a parable is to allow the parable to question you. Art functions in the same way, as it causes us to ask questions. Art also questions us. In some cases, we step into the shoes of the artist to understand what he or she may see from his or her perspective. In other cases, we imagine ourselves in the world depicted.[5] This is what has been called a heightened consciousness, "a kind of inner clarification and cleansing that refines our capacity for discernment and inclines us to respond more sensitively to the world and those around us."[6] Art stills us, quiets us, and makes us refocus and attend to what is before us.

As an opportunity for new understanding, we ask, What is the art rendering or projecting? Why was the piece conceived in the first place?[7] In admiration, we often view art's craftsmanship, attending to the dynamic of how it is done. Craftsmanship is a

---

[5] See Malcolm Guite, *Lifting the Veil: Imagination and the Kingdom of God* (London: Canterbury, 2022), 65.

[6] Kevin J. Vanhoozer, "Praising in Song: Beauty and the Arts," *The Blackwell Companion to Christian Ethics,* ed. Stanley Hauerwas and Samuel Wells (UK: John Wiley and Sons, 2011), 116.

[7] If we consider art as social discourse, we must attend to the circumstances that the piece was created in. Art is often a window into a particular time, culture, or worldview. It's an invitation to enter into that projected world. See James McCullough, *Sense and Spirituality: The Arts and Spiritual Formation* (Eugene, OR: Wipf and Stock, 2015), 8.

disciplined and acquired skill that requires practice. It involves the effective use and manipulation of the medium to communicate the intended message. Thus, before any beautiful thing is ever presented, we examine decorative patterns. We ponder what it is meant to represent, signify, or depict. We may attend to the exquisite technique, the attention to aesthetic detail, or gratefully consider how it was made to satisfy a specific need. This includes any pieces produced by an artisan like crafts, clothing, pottery, or purely decorative items. In previous generations, these were understood as art in the broadest sense, that is, as something "artificial" made by human hands.[8] Whether it is "decorative-functional" or "expressive communicative," art can take on many forms.[9] While all art shares a common aim, there is an overwhelmingly diverse expression of that pattern.[10] For this reason, art calls for a certain type of openness and attentiveness, a way of being that is also vital to our own spiritual formation.[11]

Art offers a way to grasp the world through our senses. As W. David O. Taylor notes, the arts "afford us a unique way to

---

[8] See Karen Swallow Prior, "Theology, the Arts, and Literature," in *Handbook of Theology*, ed. Daniel L. Akin, David S. Dockery, Nathan A. Finn (Brentwood, TN: B&H Academic, 2023), 620.

[9] See McCullough, *Sense and Spirituality*, 37.

[10] Adapted from John-Mark L. Miravalle, *Beauty: What It Is and Why It Matters* (Manchester, NH: Sophia Institute, 2019), 24.

[11] Francis Schaeffer's *Art and the Bible* (Downers Grove: IL: IVP, 1973) comes to mind. Schaeffer offers four standards of judgment related to art: technical excellence, validity, intellectual content, and integration of content and vehicle (62–71). Steven B. Cowan and James S. Spiegel also offer some helpful criteria in *The Love of Wisdom: A Christian Introduction to Philosophy* (Nashville: B&H Academic, 2009), 418–48.

be emotionally attuned to others, they enable us to imagine . . . and they immerse us in a sphere of metaphors by which human beings make sense of their personal and social lives."[12] As with a parable, even the most authoritative critic cannot exhaust the rich multilayered effect that art offers the recipient. There are times when art "speaks" in ways that cannot be captured in words. After all, art works on many levels to communicate while adorning and illuminating our world. Taylor suggests that art "forms our desires; it shapes our capacities to imagine the world; it confirms and disturbs our emotional instincts . . . and . . . generates a certain way of being in the world."[13] Note here that imagination is integral to our discussion. Art, like a parable, can only be "seen" through the eyes of imagination because it is through the eyes of the imagination that we are enabled to envision possibilities that are constructed from and largely remain true to the world we already know.[14] This is why it's often said that one can visit a distant land when reading a beautiful narrative. When contemplating a painting, one can travel through time and learn the values of cultures long gone through their accessories and aesthetic ornamentation. When listening to a song, one can enter the opened heart of the artist and understand that artist's experiences. This is all possible because art doesn't just tell a story; it also shapes our vision of the world, even if indirectly. Thus, imagination is not just at the heart of all

---

[12] W. David O. Taylor, *Glimpses of the New Creation: Worship and the Formative Power of the Arts* (Grand Rapids: Eerdmans, 2019), 4.

[13] Taylor, *Glimpses of the New Creation*, 1–2.

[14] See Oliver Davies, *The Creativity of God: World, Eucharist, Reason* (Cambridge, UK: Cambridge University Press, 2004), 57.

artistic making, it is essential to our awareness and integral to training our eyes to see.[15]

Art as Beauty for Ashes

Art requires a certain ability to transcend oneself to see things in a different light, perhaps as it truly is, or even how it is meant to be. Stanley Hauerwas says that "great art show[s] us our world with a clarity which startles us because we are not used to looking at the real world at all."[16] Any honest appraisal of life in this fallen world will confront us with imperfection. For this reason, artists cannot ignore the lingering questions of the day. This is why art with a "Pollyanna" quality to it often comes off as shallow and trivial; it strikes us as untrue. Unfortunately, much of what might be called "Christian art" falls into this category, ignoring the complexity and brokenness of our world. Furthermore, Christians have often found it hard to appreciate art that does not supply an explicitly spiritual conclusion.[17] In contrast, great art that reaches the depths of our hearts is often

---

[15] See Matt 4:16; and Guite, *Lifting the Veil*, 20. Imagination, like art, has often been seen as suspect by some Christians who perceive the art world as an assault upon traditional values. These explanations of art are largely driven by fear that art will lead us away from "truth" into an anarchic freedom of expression (see Fujimura, *Art + Faith*, 5). "Attention" is prominent in the writings of Simone Weil. For example, see *Waiting for God* (New York: Harper, 2009).

[16] Stanley Hauerwas, "The Significance of Vision: Toward an Aesthetic Ethic," *Sciences Religieuses/Studies in Religion* 2 (1972): 38.

[17] Steve Turner addresses this in his work *Imagine* by offering a set of differentiating qualities that allow Christians to appreciate art that dignifies human life and introduces a sense of awe, carries an imprint of clear Bible teaching even if it's not explicitly Christian, or is inspired by the Bible's primary theological themes. Steve Turner, *Imagine: A*

born from struggle or pain, either from the painstakingly tedious process of creation, its delicate subject matter, or its moving message. Indeed, the great artists are often the most sensitive to the world around them and can capture the great joys or troubling struggles of life with a profound depth. Being confronted with the brokenness of our current world is one of the ways our assumptions and complacency can be challenged. On the other hand, for the Christian, being provoked to anticipate the world to come is one way our souls are renewed as our loves and desires are rightly indexed.[18] In this way, "art has the redemptive power to take into account humanity's suffering while at the same time showing us the hope of healing."[19] Christian artists in particular have the unique perspective to both acknowledge suffering while preserving hope.[20]

We could say then that art is analogous to the Spirit's wordless groans of anticipation (Rom 8:22, 26). Our imaginations must come to be, in a sense, baptized for us to grasp "the *in-betweenness*, the something good and the 'something missing,' of our lives in the fallen world."[21] On this point, it is worth quoting John-Mark Hart at length:

Vision for Christians in the Arts (Downers Grove, IL: InterVarsity, 2017), 104–14.

[18] In a sense, we could also point to the marks inscribed upon the flesh of the resurrected Lord. He ascended to heaven bearing the marks of earthly pain. See Bruce Herman, "Wounds and Beauty," in Daniel J. Treier, Mark Husbands, and Roger Lundin, *The Beauty of God: Theology and the Arts*, 111, 118. Quoted in Ryken, 126.

[19] Ryken, *Beauty Is Your Destiny*, 74.

[20] E. John Walford, "The Case for Broken Beauty: An Art Historical Viewpoint," in *The Beauty of God: Theology and the Arts*, ed. Daniel J. Treier, Mark Husbands, and Roger Lundin (Downers Grove IL: IVP Academic, 2007), 109.

[21] Myers, *A Poetics of Orthodoxy*, 54.

> All human art between Adam's fall and Christ's second advent must be shaped at some level by mourning for the world's brokenness and hope for the world's healing. Art that is not attuned to the ugliness and brokenness of much in the present world order will generally either fail to speak to us in any meaningful way or somehow mask the world's brokenness by portraying it as good. Conversely, art that neither sees any value in the world nor evokes any vision of truth, beauty, and goodness that transcend the world in its present state will generally cultivate despair. But great art shapes us in manifold ways to live beautifully in the world as it is while maintaining our awareness that a better world is possible. For the Christian, this awareness of a better world takes the form of deep assurance that God will unite all things in Christ and fill the new earth with the glory of his eternal truth, beauty, and goodness. Creating and enjoying such art is an expression of authentic human vocation and an important part of the church's participation in the beauty of God that is being disclosed in his redemption of the world.[22]

Attending to Art

The world needs beauty now more than ever before. We could ask, as Karen Swallow Prior does, "Should we make time for art" alongside the church's call to evangelize and make disciples? And "Do the works of human hands and mortal minds really

[22] John-Mark Hart, "Triune Beauty and the Ugly Cross: Towards a Theological Aesthetic," *Tyndale Bulletin* 66, no. 2 (2015): 311.

matter in the face of eternity?"[23] We would wholeheartedly affirm so! Indeed, art has always been part of the warp and woof of the human experience. The call to create is embedded in our composition as God's image bearers. Art is for the good of mankind because aesthetic invention has always played "a large part . . . in man's effort to build a meaningful world."[24] As Pope John Paul II once wrote in a letter to artists, "Society needs artists, just as it needs scientists, technicians, workers, professional people . . . who ensure the growth of the person and the development of the community."[25]

It remains true that the fallen nature of the world makes it possible for the arts to have an immoral effect on an audience and even vexes the artistic task under the duress of sin (Exod 32:1–24; Rom 1:21–23). We should also note the precarious relationship between the arts and worship, especially in our culture where art has become "art for art's sake, a kind of irreligious religion."[26] As Christians, we understand that art is not an end in itself, lest it become a false idol. Even with these cautions, we should not be deterred from receiving God's good gifts of the earth with gladness and fashioning them aesthetically toward noble ends. By God's common grace, Christians are still able to do much in the areas of beauty and aesthetics. Wayne Grudem

---

[23] Prior, "Theology, the Arts, and Literature," 619.

[24] Lewis Mumford, *The Myth of the Machine: Technics and Human Development* (New York: Harcourt, Brace and World, 1966), 153.

[25] "Letter of His Holiness Pope John Paul II to Artists," 1999, no. 4, on the website of the Vatican, https://www.vatican.va/content/john-paul-ii/en/letters/1999/documents/hf_jp-ii_let_23041999_artists.html.

[26] Hans R. Rookmaker, *Art Needs No Justification* (Downers Grove, IL: InterVarsity, 1978), 13.

argues, "The more Christian influence there is in a society in general, the more clearly the influence of common grace will be seen in the lives of unbelievers as well."[27]

This conviction is one of the reasons the church has been one of the primary sponsors of the arts throughout history.[28] The Christian tradition has always provided a river of creativity and beauty flowing out into the world. One of Michelangelo's best-known works was commissioned directly by the church. Raphael worked in and on various churches and cathedrals. Many of Handel's musical compositions were directly tied to biblical texts and themes. Dostoevsky's novels often mirrored his own journey through sensuality and skepticism toward the faith. Indeed, "if we are to understand beauty's presence or absence in the long history of the Christian movement, we cannot simply ignore the arts. . . . Beauty has always been an intrinsic part of Christian liturgy and celebratory festivals."[29]

Art and Eternal Endurance

Art, like any other worthwhile human endeavor, both expresses the experiences and also addresses the longings of mankind. It makes us aware of the gulf between our eternal longings and the actual world of our dwelling. Even more, while the beauty of any created good is only provisional and partial, it has within it an enduring testimony that reverberates into eternity.[30] There is consequently

---

[27] Wayne Grudem, *Systematic Theology: An Introduction to Biblical Doctrine* (Grand Rapids: Zondervan, 2009), 497.

[28] See Turner, *Imagine*, 35–36.

[29] Edward Farley, *Faith and Beauty: A Theological Aesthetic*, Ashgate Studies in Theology, Imagination and the Arts (Abingdon, UK: Ashgate, 2001), 6.

[30] Miravalle, *Beauty*, 75.

strong encouragement to believe that our thirst for beauty will be satisfied. Karl Heim explains, "Every really great piece of music, every great work of art therefore is the morning light of eternity, a first dawn of the perfecting of the world. Immortal works of music, classical works of art are like the fir trees on the slopes of the mountain, whose tops are already in the light of the approaching morning while the valley is still covered in mist."[31]

We cannot forget that a biblical worldview teaches us that creation gives way to new creation. In the end, the consummating kiln of God's judgment will burn away the dross, but what is good, true, and beautiful will endure.[32] Thus, the hope of eternity should not mark a complete break with earthly experience but instead should intensify all that is good with the addition of unimaginable new dimensions.[33] As Fujimura has argued, "What we build, design, and depict on this side of eternity matters, because in some mysterious way, those creations will become part of the future city of God."[34] I don't think it is a coincidence that gold, which could be dug up from the bed of a river exiting Eden, is later refined and used to cover the walls and streets of the Holy City in the new creation (Gen 2:12; Rev 21:18–21). Even in the earthen materials we use to create, there is a continuity that stretches into eternity. Thus, in the act of making, according to N. T. Wright, we accomplish something that will become in due course part of God's new world. Wright maintains that "every

---

[31] Karl Heim, *Jesus, the World's Perfecter: The Atonement and the Renewal of the World*, trans. D. H. van Daalen, American ed. (Philadelphia: Muhlenberg, 1961), 1996.

[32] This is the work of transformation, bringing forth a new concept of what already is (2 Cor 5:17).

[33] See Turner, *Imagine*, 77.

[34] Fujimura, *Art + Faith*, 12.

work of art or music inspired by the love of God and delight in the beauty of his creation . . . every deed that . . . builds up the church . . . will find its way, through the resurrecting power of God, into the new creation that God will one day make."[35]

It has been said that when attending to or contemplating great art, we enter the antechamber of heaven and stand on eternity's very brink.[36] I am reminded once again of Augustine's argument that our hearts are restless until they rest in God. Remember, for several of the church fathers, to be human is to be oriented toward God, who is the chief object of our love.[37] And the greatest theological virtue is love (1 Cor 13:13)! It is curious then that, of the transcendentals, it could be argued that beauty has a particular way of stirring the affections, perhaps more effectively than truth or goodness. In this sense, all earthly beauties are a glimpse, like the first breathtaking but distant sight of one's future spouse, by which we are drawn in to the "beauty of all things beautiful."[38]

A Call to Attend to the Arts

Remember, as the body of Christ, we are the embodiment of the divine life in the world. For this reason, artists should be active in creating works that not only allow recipients to experience

---

[35] N. T. Wright, *Surprised by Hope: Rethinking Heaven, the Resurrection, and the Misson of the Church* (Grand Rapids: Zondervan, 2008), 208.

[36] See Vanhoozer, "Praising in Song."

[37] See Augustine's *Confessions* (1.1.1) or Irenaeus' *Against Heresies* (4.20.7).

[38] Augustine, *Confessions* (3.6.10). Gerald O'Collins, *Christology: A Biblical, Historical, and Systematic Study of Jesus* (Oxford, UK: Oxford University Press, 2009), 314.

a contemplative encounter with our hurting world but also awaken a transcendent longing for the world to come. In addition to making art, Christians must be the most enthusiastic appreciators of art insofar as we see it as an expression of the God-given vocation. As we have seen, art has a way of moving through the senses into the soul. The mystery of faith calls artists as well as theologians to the table. Perhaps we should say, artists as theologians.

Let us then reclaim creativity as essential to the faith journey. After all, the gift to cultivate beautiful things was given to us by the Creator as a capacity to steward, and it is a gift that no other creature under heaven possesses. Art's justification is that it is itself a potential given by God. Art creates an atmosphere in which we live; it gives us words to speak; it offers us a framework in which we can see and grasp things, "say a landscape, even without noticing it."[39] It is a shame, then, that beauty and aesthetics have so often been neglected by the church, being viewed as ornamental and not as constitutive of the Christian faith.[40] After all, without attending to aesthetics, we run the risk of being color-blind to the grandeur of God's world and thus to his glory. If God is the embodiment of true and perfect beauty, then it is our task to contemplate and respond in worshipful adoration of what has been drawn by him.

---

[39] Rookmaker, *Art Needs No Justification*, 35.

[40] Brad Harper and Paul Louis Metzger, *Exploring Ecclesiology: An Evangelical and Ecumenical Introduction* (Eugene, OR: Brazos, 2009), 235.

APPENDIX

Coming to Art with Your Senses

Aesthetic Awareness for Art Appreciation

> Finally brothers and sisters, whatever is true, whatever is honorable, whatever is just, whatever is pure, whatever is lovely [beautiful], whatever is commendable—if there is any moral excellence and if there is anything praiseworthy—dwell on these things.
>
> —*Philippians* 4:8

Dwelling on What Is Beautiful

Throughout this book, I have helped you build a theological scaffolding for beauty, aesthetics, and spiritual formation. Now I would like to help you work out Paul's encouragement in Phil 4:8 in regard to appreciating art. One of the things the apostle exhorted his readers to practice in this passage is "dwelling on" or "taking into account" what is "lovely" or "beautiful." That is, dwell on things that are pleasing or agreeable.

Broadly speaking, Paul is addressing things that commend themselves by their intrinsic attractiveness because they are like a delightful fragrance to the soul. The idea of "dwelling" on something implies a receptivity or consent to "anything praiseworthy." We will apply this principle in a broader sense to things in art that we might find beautiful or aesthetically pleasing (see Eccl 3:11 NIV).

In relation to artistic creation, all artists "add to the world" by using the elements God gave us to develop and beautify our existence. Even more, art is meant to—in some way or another—enrich the lives of those who experience it. Artists have given us a vast treasury of paintings, music, poetry, photographs, architecture, and sculptures to experience and enjoy. The question is, How are we to approach art with attentiveness and grow in aesthetic appreciation? Even if one finds the worldview of the artist or content of the piece disagreeable, there may be elements of the piece that can still be appreciated.

Experiencing Art with Our Senses

What follows is a guide to examine art in general, understanding that there is beauty found in art done by non-Christians and Christians, and in explicitly Christian art. When we refer to Christian art, it means that one's faith is communicated as a major or minor theme in the piece or that it is Christian in the broad or narrow sense—either communicating a biblical scene or a theological truth in some way or another.[1] So then, how do

---

[1] See Hans R. Rookmaker, *Art Needs No Justification* (Vancouver: Regent College, 2010) for a booklet-length treatment on this idea. Steve Turner also offers the imagery of concentric circles where the

we appreciate what is lovely or beautiful in each piece of art? Allow me to offer a few categories to help us to come with our senses when experiencing art.[2]

Consent

Artists communicate by expression, while recipients receive through impression. The recipient always has a posture of consent. The most receptive disposition for the beholder is that of attentiveness. Remember, consent is the relationship between the artist and/or object to the beholder. Consent implies a dialogue in which the recipient may enter and participate. The first step in coming to art with your senses is to take your time and attentively examine a piece of art in its totality, to unhurriedly open yourself to the impact of the work.

Craftsmanship

Second, the observant patron understands that every piece of art is made of different elements or ingredients. The patron understands that attentiveness to these details and how those

---

outer ring represents art that does not suggest a worldview, in the next circle a piece may suggest a theme related to the faith, in the third ring is art that contains an imprint of a clear Christian teaching, the inner circle is made up of explicitly Christian art, that is pieces that hold forth a primary biblical theme or depict theological imagery. See Turner, *Imagine: A Vision for Christians in the Arts* (Downers Grove, IL: InterVarsity, 2017), 104–10).

[2] The headers for the last three categories are adapted from James McCullough's *Sense and Spirituality: The Arts and Spiritual Formation* (Eugene, OR: Wipf and Stock, 2015).

details work together shape the patron's experience of the piece as a whole.[3] Craftsmanship involves the successful use of materials or elements to communicate effectively or to affect one deeply. Excellency in craft is a disciplined or acquired skill based on the technical excellence employed by the artist, and in turn this relates to the quality or impact of the work.[4] Thus, one might closely examine how the artist utilizes different elements (things like brushstrokes, instrumentation, spacing, colors, contrast, chisel patterns). Or one might consider how effectively the artist executes the craft in the tradition of style or practice of the medium being used.

Content

Third, as James McCullough contends, one must understand that "meaningful and informative encounters with art inevitably involve the processes of interpretation."[5] All art tells a story or communicates a message in some way or another. Art can be a window into the culture and worldview of the artist, a window the recipient is invited to see through. Art can also function to smash the windows through which we view the world, confronting our own perspectives, assumptions, or biases. Art can also introduce us to or surprise us in new ways of appreciating or understanding. We might then ask, Is there an observable

[3] Elissa Yukiko Weichbrodt's *Redeeming Vision: A Christian Guide to Looking at and Learning from Art* (Grand Rapids: Baker Academic, 2023) is an excellent guide for understanding how we can experience and interpret art on a deeper level.

[4] See Francis Schaeffer, *Art and the Bible* (Downers Grove, IL: IVP, 2006), 62–63.

[5] McCullough, *Sense and Spirituality*, 30.

sequence or flow within the composition that informs us of the piece's focal point or climax? What is being communicated or evoked by the imagery, tone, metaphor, or movement of the piece?[6] If possible, we might consider the craftsmanship and content together and ask how well the medium or style chosen is suited for the intended message.[7]

Context

Finally, for further reflection, it is generally helpful to educate yourself on the piece under consideration.[8] Any level of information or research available will help you better understand the piece itself, the author's intent behind it, and sometimes the culture and time in which it was produced. Every artist creates at a certain point in history, and the cultural values of that time—along with the beliefs and prejudices of that moment—are often embodied in the work. More personally, all artists have a story, and their experience of their world is often reflected in their work. Even more, understanding the time and culture in which art was created allows one to grow in appreciation of the artist's craft, especially in older works where certain technologies were not yet available.

---

[6] A couple of works of note that exemplify this type of analysis are Benjamin P. Myers's *A Poetics of Orthodoxy: Christian Truth as Aesthetic Foundation* (Eugene, OR: Wipf and Stock, 2020) and Malcolm Guite's *Lifting the Veil: Imagination and the Kingdom of God* (London: Canterbury, 2022).

[7] See Schaeffer, *Art and the Bible*, 69–71.

[8] Russ Ramsey demonstrates how to do this well in his book *Rembrandt Is in the Wind: Learning to Love Art through the Eyes of Faith* (Grand Rapids: Zondervan, 2022).

Conclusion

In the end, the Christian understands that all that we appreciate in art as beautiful or lovely is transitory, like a lingering scent that leads us toward the One who is the source and substance of all good things. Works of art are good images of what we truly desire.[9] They are but a taste of what we will one day fully see, the goodness of our God. Aesthetic experiences can serve as effective servants to our spiritual formation, if we learn to be attentive. Art can be a gift that makes us aware of God's goodness in our world and helps us see his goodness in our lives. Remember the words of John-Mark Hart: "God has made us embodied, sensory beings in a world that is teeming with holy and delightful sights, sounds, smells, and tastes that are among those good gifts descending from above for which we should give thanks."[10] Let us give thanks to the God whose beauty draws us to him.

"Everything comes from you, and we have given you
only what comes from your hand."
1 Chronicles 29:14 (NIV)

---

[9] See C. S. Lewis, *The Weight of Glory* (New York: Macmillan, 1966), 4–5.

[10] John-Mark Hart, "Triune Beauty and the Ugly Cross: Towards a Theological Aesthetic," *Tyndale Bulletin* 66, no. 2 (2015): 305.

AUTHOR INDEX

SUBJECT INDEX

D

E

F

G

O

P

R

S

Y

Z

SCRIPTURE INDEX